COLLINS PC

WRITTEN
DRIVING TEST

Philip Coyne
and
The National Extension College

HarperCollins*Publishers*

HarperCollins Publishers
P.O. Box, Glasgow G4 ONB

First published 1996

Reprint 10 9 8 7 6 5 4 3 2 1

ISBN 0 00 470986 1

This book was written by Philip Coyne for the National Extension College.

The National Extension College is an educational trust and registered charity with a distinguished body of trustees. It is an independent, self-financing organisation.
  Since it was established in 1963, NEC has pioneered the development of flexible learning for adults. NEC is actively developing innovative materials and systems for distance-learning options from basic skills and general education to degree level as well as vocational and professional training and education.

Philip Coyne is an expert writer on driving and wrote *Roadcraft: The Police Driving Manual* and *Motorcycle Roadcraft* for NEC.

A catalogue record for this book is available from the British Library

Printed and bound in Great Britain by Caledonian International Book Manufacturing Ltd, Glasgow G64

Contents

Introduction

The theory test was introduced in July 1996 to comply with a European Community directive aimed at improving driver training. The test is designed to assess whether you have the necessary understanding and knowledge to drive safely. *Collins Pocket Reference Written Driving Test* takes you step by step through all the topics covered by the test. If you know this book and the Highway Code well, and you follow the book's advice on tackling multiple choice questions, you will be well prepared to take the test.

TEN KEY PRINCIPLES FOR SAFE DRIVING

These ten principles give good advice covering many different driving situations. Although you will not be tested on the ten principles as such, they summarise much of the knowledge on which you will be tested.

1 Get your attitude right
- don't take unnecessary risks
- don't compete with other drivers
- don't let yourself get angry
- don't be aggressive
- be tolerant, courteous and helpful.

2 Concentrate on your driving
- don't allow your attention to wander or allow yourself to be distracted
- observe, anticipate, assess, decide, act.

3 Observe and anticipate
- look well ahead so you know what to expect
- know what is happening all round you
- check your mirrors regularly
- check your mirrors whenever you see a hazard
- check your mirrors whenever you change speed or direction
- check your blind spots
- anticipate the possible hazards in areas you cannot see into
- anticipate the actions of other road users.

4 Adapt to the conditions
- weather
- visibility
- other road users
- junctions, bends, hills and slope of the road
- road layout and road surface.

5 Get your position right
- position away from danger
- position so you can see
- position so others can see you
- position for stability
- follow the vehicle in front at a safe distance.

Right-hand bend: *approach and go round the bend well to the left to get the best view of the road ahead.*

Left-hand bend: *approach and go round the bend in the middle of your lane.*

6 Get your speed right

- adapt your speed to the conditions
- know your safe stopping distances
- always be able to stop in the distance you can see to be clear.

7 Get the gear right

- anticipate the gear that you will need so that you always have the power to drive out of danger.

8 Brake on the straight, steer on the bends

- avoid braking and steering at the same time
- reduce your speed on the approach to a bend so that you do not have to brake and steer at the same time
- steer and brake smoothly.

9 Signal your intentions clearly

- use the correct signals
- signal when other road users could benefit
- signal early enough for other road users to respond.

10 Know and use the Highway Code

- know the regulations that apply to your vehicle
- know the rules for different types of roads
- know the correct signals
- know road signs and markings
- obey instructions and follow advice.

KEY TERMS

A few words occur frequently in the text and have specialised meanings. It is as well to be clear what they mean from the start:

MUST and MUST NOT

In the Highway Code the words MUST and MUST NOT refer to what is required by law. We use them in the same way in this book when talking about rules and regulations on the road. So, for example, where we have written 'You MUST stop at a **'Stop'** sign', this means that the law requires you to do this. Not to stop is an offence.

Nearside and offside

These identify which side of a vehicle you are talking about. When you sit in the driving seat of a vehicle looking forwards, the nearside is on the left and the offside is on the right. The words also apply to the road. Facing in the direction of the traffic flow, the left side of the road is the nearside, the right side of the road is the offside.

Observation

To drive safely, you need to know what is going on all round you. Carefully looking all round to gather essential information is called observation. You need to be aware at all times of what is happening:

- in the distance
- in the mid-ground
- immediately in front of you
- to the sides
- behind you.

It requires you to keep your eyes moving (see scanning), to use your mirrors frequently and to pay attention to what you can hear and smell as well as what you can see.

Other road user

This phrase emphasises the need to be aware that the roads are used for a range of purposes and are not for the sole use of those driving vehicles. These other road users, for example pedestrians, cyclists, motorcyclists and horse riders, have particular needs and vulnerabilities that must be taken into account by vehicle drivers.

Scanning

This is a way of using your eyes to improve your observation. Use regular sweeps of your eyes to scan the whole of the road – in front, to the sides and behind. Avoid staring at one spot for a long time. A common mistake is not to look far enough ahead. When you look in front, make sure you look at what is happening in the distance and in the mid-ground as well as at what is happening immediately in front of you. Use your mirrors regularly, and always before you change course or speed.

This way of keeping your eyes constantly on the move helps you to build a full picture of what is going on around you. It improves your awareness, and helps you to identify hazards early.

1 Getting organised

Before you can take your practical driving test, you need to pass the theory test. You then have up to two years in which to pass the practical test. If you do not pass a practical test within two years, you must start again and take a new theory test.

You cannot drive on the road on your own until you have passed both parts of the test. To book and sit the theory test you must have a valid provisional driving licence. Use the checklist below to help you plan.

ARRANGING TO TAKE THE THEORY TEST

Get a provisional licence

- Get a provisional licence application form D1 from the post office, Traffic Area Office, Vehicle Registration Office or Driver and Vehicle Licensing Authority (DVLA).

- Fill in the form and send it with the fee (£21 in 1996) to the Driver and Vehicle Licensing Authority in Swansea. You should receive your provisional licence within three weeks. Sign the licence when you receive it. A provisional licence is then valid until your 70th birthday.

Plan how long it will take you to study for the theory test

• Plan how you will prepare for the theory and practical tests.

• If you can, organise some practical driving experience while you are studying for the theory test.

• Decide when you think you will be ready to pass the theory test.

Book your test date

The earliest date you can be offered is three days from when you book, but you may have to wait longer. The earlier you book the more likely you are to get the date you want.

• Get a theory test application form from your local driving test centre, theory test centre, the theory test booking and enquiry office or your driving instructor.

• Send off the form to the theory test booking office with the fee (£15 in 1996). If you book by post you should receive details of your test appointment within ten days.

• You can book by telephone by using a credit or debit card on 0645 000666.

• You should receive a test appointment within ten days of booking by post.

What you are required to take to the theory test centre

• Your signed provisional driving licence

• Your booking number (sent to you with your test appointment)

• Some form of independent identification.

Your licence and identity will be checked before you can take the test.

The test centre

• Theory test centres have a reception and waiting area, toilets (with disabled facilities where possible), an examination room and a separate area for those who need special help with taking the test.

• You will be supervised while you sit the test.

• You cannot take any books or papers into the exam room.

• You will be given a pen and the question paper and told when to start.

• You have 40 minutes for the test. The exam room has a clock and you will be told when there is five minutes left.

• You cannot take the question paper or any other material away from the test.

• You will be asked to answer 35 multiple choice questions. You have to answer 26 questions correctly to pass the test.

• You will receive your test results within about a week.

THE TEST QUESTIONS

You will be tested from a bank of questions drawn up by the Driving Standards Agency (DSA). The DSA have published 435 of these questions, applicable to cars, in the book *The complete theory test for cars and motorcycles*. This book contains all the questions that you are likely to be asked in the test. From time to time the questions will be revised.

The questions in the test will be in the form of multiple choice questions. These give a question followed by several possible answers. You have to tick the correct answer. Generally you are required to tick only one answer, but some questions ask you to tick two or more answers. It is important to follow the instructions for each question very carefully.

Multiple choice questions

Answering multiple choice questions may seem quite easy, but bear the following in mind.

- The theory test is carefully designed to test your knowledge – it won't be easy to guess the right answers.

- The wrong choices are called 'distracters'. They can be very confusing. They are put in the test to check common mistakes in understanding.

- Unless you know what the question is testing, several of the choices may seem equally probable.

How to tackle multiple choice questions

• Always stick closely to what is given in the question.

• Do not bring in ideas outside of what is given in the question.

• Do not overlook important information given in the question.

• Look for the answer that follows most closely from what is given.

• Mark your answers in the way required. Put a cross clearly against the answer you choose. An unclear mark may be discounted. If you are asked to mark one answer and you mark more than one, your answer will be incorrect.

• If you change your mind, blank out the incorrect box completely with your pen.

• Follow the instructions. Some questions ask you to mark more than one answer. If you mark only one, you will lose the mark for that question.

• Allow enough time for each question, so that you don't have to rush later questions. Each question carries only one mark, so it isn't worth puzzling over any single question for too long.

GETTING ON THE ROAD

Note

Where the words 'must' or 'must not' are used in this book, they are legal requirements.

Before learning to drive on a public highway you are legally required to:
• have the necessary documents
• be medically fit to drive
• display L plates on the vehicle (or a D plate in Wales)
• be supervised by an appropriately experienced driver.

Documents

Before driving on the public highway, drivers are legally required to be covered by the following documents, valid at the time of driving:
• a driving licence – a provisional driving licence for those who have not passed the test
• a vehicle excise licence (tax disc)
• a certificate of motor insurance
• a vehicle test certificate if the car is over three years old (MOT).

Medical fitness

You must be medically fit to drive. If you have a medical condition which could affect your driving, you must tell the Driving and Vehicle Licensing

Authority. The driving licence application form lists the conditions that you must tell them about. If you do not tell the DVLA about a relevant illness or disability, your licence may not be valid.

L plates

If you hold a provisional licence, you must display 'L' plates or, in Wales, 'D' plates. D is for 'dysgwr' which is Welsh for 'learner'.

Supervision

Holders of provisional driving licences must be supervised while driving on a public road by a driver who:

• is over 21

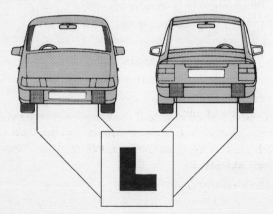

Where to position L-plates

- holds a full driving licence which is valid for driving cars
- has held a full licence, valid for cars, for at least three years.

If you pay someone to supervise you, they must be an Approved Driving Instructor (ADI) or Trainee Licence holder.

THE PROVISIONAL DRIVING LICENCE

You must have a valid provisional licence before you learn to drive on a public road.

- Remember to sign it, otherwise it is not valid.
- Remember you are required to take your signed provisional licence with you to both the theory and the practical test.
- A provisional licence for a car is valid until your 70th birthday.

Your licence gives:
- your driver number
- your address. You must inform the Driving and Vehicle Licensing Authority (DVLA) if you change your address
- details of any endorsements.

THE VEHICLE EXCISE LICENCE
– TAX DISC

• Your vehicle must display a valid excise licence,
  usually referred to as a tax disc.

• The tax disc shows the make, model, registration
  number and class of vehicle, and the date the licence
  expires.

You can get a tax disc at main post offices. You cannot
obtain a disc unless you can present:
• a completed application form, normally sent to you
  by the DVLA when a new licence is due, or available
  at post offices if you buy a new car
• a current certificate of motor insurance
• a current MOT certificate, if the car is over three
  years old (or four years in Northern Ireland).

THE CERTIFICATE OF MOTOR
INSURANCE

You must be insured for driving. Cover may be
provided by your own personal policy or someone
else's policy. If you are driving under somone else's
policy you must make sure you are covered by it.
Policies vary widely. Someone else's policy may give
you no cover at all or only cover for third party risks.

The certificate of motor insurance states:
• who is insured

- what type of vehicle is covered
- what kind of risks are insured
- when the insurance cover starts and ends.

Types of motor insurance

Third party

- This is the minimum legal cover.
- It is the cheapest.
- It covers you if you injure another person or damage another person's property.
- It doesn't cover you if you damage your vehicle or injure yourself.

Third party, fire and theft

- This is more expensive than third party but provides more cover.
- This covers you if your vehicle is stolen or damaged by fire.
- It includes third party cover.

Comprehensive

- This is the most expensive but provides the widest cover.
- It includes third party, fire and theft.
- It covers you if you damage your vehicle, injure yourself or need replacement parts after accident damage.

THE VEHICLE TEST CERTIFICATE (MOT)

This is a compulsory safety check that all vehicles over three years old (four years old in Northern Ireland) must undergo once a year. If the vehicle passes it will receive a vehicle test certificate, usually known as an MOT certificate. (The test is known as the MOT because it was introduced by the old Ministry of Transport.)

The MOT test checks:

• the safety components of your car, for example brakes, brake pipes, headlights, sidelights, brakelights, indicators and seat belts

• the level of harmful gases (emissions) from the exhaust.

The test does not check the state of the engine, clutch or gearbox. The test certificate is valid for 12 months, but this does not necessarily mean your car will remain safe for this period. You should carry out regular safety checks.

You cannot renew the vehicle tax disc for a car older than three years without a valid test certificate. And you must not drive a car over three years old (four years old in Northern Ireland) on a public road without a valid test certificate. The only exceptions are:

• when driving a vehicle to a test appointment.

- driving a failed vehicle away from the test station
- driving a failed vehicle to a garage to correct the defects identified in the test.

KEEPING YOUR DOCUMENTS SAFE

- You should keep your documents in a safe place.
- In the UK you do not have to carry them in your car, or on your person. In fact, both car and documents are more secure if you don't.
- Keep documents somewhere safe but accessible at home so they can easily be produced if required.

Providing information to the police and other people

A uniformed police officer has the power to ask you to produce your documents.

- If you do not have them with you, the police officer will ask you to present them at a police station of your choice within seven days.
- Not do to so is an offence.

The only times when you must show your documents to other people are:

- if you are involved in an accident where someone is injured. You must show your insurance certificate to anyone who has reasonable grounds to ask for it, if you have it with you. (Otherwise you must produce it within 24 hours to the police.)

• when you renew your vehicle's tax disc. You must show your certificate of motor insurance and MOT certificate if the vehicle is over three years old (four years old in Northern Ireland).

THE VEHICLE REGISTRATION DOCUMENT

This document contains key information about a vehicle. It does not necessarily prove ownership. The following information is on the document:

• the name and address of the registered keeper of the vehicle

• the vehicle registration number – the number on the number plate

• the make, colour and class of vehicle

• the vehicle identification number, which is stamped on the vehicle body

• the engine size and engine number.

At the bottom of the form there is a slip which you have to complete if the vehicle is sold or passed to another person.

2 Your attitude to driving

Research shows that our attitudes significantly affect our safety as drivers. You can reduce your risk of having an accident by developing the right attitudes. For example, young men are involved in twice as many fatal accidents as young women because young men drive faster. By altering their attitude to speed, young men could reduce their risk of dying in a road accident.

Our safety as drivers is affected by our attitudes to:
• speed
• risk-taking
• other road users
• emotional reactions
• positive thinking.

SPEED

Excess speed is one of the major causes of accidents. The faster you go the less time you have to react. Drivers who regularly speed are more likely to have an accident. You should always:
• drive at a speed appropriate for the circumstances
• be able to stop in the distance you can see to be clear
• keep a safe following distance between yourself and the vehicle in front

• adjust your speed according to the weather, visibility,
  road and surface conditions and the presence of other
  road users.

RISK-TAKING

Obviously, the more risks we take the more likely we
are to have an accident. Seeking thrills from driving
endangers your own life, the lives of your passengers
and the lives of other road users. You need to be able
to recognise when you are taking risks for the sake of
the thrill, and to stop yourself from doing it. The roads
are risky enough, without creating unnecessary risks.

Another major cause of accidents is failing to
recognise when situations are hazardous. Low hazard
awareness is a major cause of accidents for new
drivers. Developing your awareness of the likely
hazards is an important part of learning to drive. This
is covered in **4 Recognising hazards**.

OTHER ROAD USERS

Safe use of the road depends on cooperation. It is only
by observing common conventions, such as which side
of the road to drive on, that traffic can move freely at
all. We need to understand the needs of other road
users and adapt our behaviour to meet these needs. To
do this you need to know the Highway Code
thoroughly and to appreciate the needs of other road

users. **5 Vulnerable road users** and **10 Other vehicles** will help you to do this.

EMOTIONAL REACTIONS

Emotional reactions affect your judgement and encourage you to take unnecessary risks. The main negative emotions you need to guard against are:

• time stress
• anger
• aggression
• competition.

Your emotional mood affects your driving. If you have recently suffered a bereavement, unhappy separation or some other emotional trauma it will affect your concentration and judgement. Short-term emotional disturbances, such as arguments with your partner, employer or colleagues will undermine your driving ability. With short-term upsets, take time to cool off and regain composure before you drive. With more fundamental emotional disturbances you should drive more slowly and build extra safety margins into your driving.

Time stress

Time stress, the feeling that you have to be somewhere by a specific time, is a major hazard. It encourages:

• speeding

- risk-taking
- disregard for other road users.

If you are going to be late, just accept that you will be late. It is not worth risking lives to be punctual.

- Allow sufficient time for your journey.
- Allow extra time if weather or road conditions are poor.
- If you fall behind schedule, accept that you are going to be late.

Anger

If you get angry with another motorist, you are not in a fit state to drive. Pull over and wait till you have calmed down before continuing. Do not risk lives just because someone cut you up. Disengage, try to look at the situation calmly – regard reckless drivers as just one more hazard that you have to take into account.

Aggression

Aggression has no place on the road. There are enough hazards on the road already without adding unnecessary hazards. Don't get involved in aggression; the stakes are too high.

Competition

Competition is dangerous on the road. Competition causes you to take risks and leads to aggression and anger. If you feel yourself starting to compete, recognise what you are doing and don't get caught up in it.

POSITIVE THINKING

In contrast to these negative emotions try to develop the positive attitudes of:

• tolerance
• consideration
• courtesy.

These attitudes are safer and help you to make better use of the roads.

Tolerance

Tolerance is essential for safe driving on Britain's crowded roads. Take for example the situation where someone pulls out in front of you at a junction, forcing you to brake

• Do not retaliate.
• Slow down and be prepared to stop.
• Follow at a safe distance.
• Do not allow yourself to get irritated.

Show tolerance. It could quite easily have been a mistake and even if it wasn't, you gain nothing by responding aggressively.

Consideration

Show consideration for other road users by:

• anticipating their needs

• showing patience

• giving way, even when you have priority

• showing courtesy.

Insisting on your own priority can be dangerous. One in four accidents occur when someone drives across another driver's priority. Be understanding of other road users' needs and try to assist them.

Courtesy

Being courteous improves your own state of mind and affects the attitudes of other drivers as well.

• If you make a mistake, apologise for it.

• If someone gives way, thank them for it.

• If you are in a slow-moving vehicle and traffic builds up behind you, find a safe place to pull in and let the other vehicles pass.

The road can be a stressful place. Showing courtesy helps to diffuse the stress and makes the roads safer for everyone.

3 Alertness and impairment

The more alert we are, the better we are able to
perform skilled tasks like driving, and the safer we are
likely to be. So we need to be alert when we drive.
But equally we need to avoid things which undermine
our alertness – those things which impair alertness. To
do this we need to know what they are.

ALERTNESS

Safe driving depends on gathering information about
road and traffic conditions and acting on it
appropriately. The amount of information that we are
able to cope with depends on how alert we are. Even a
split-second lapse in concentration could cause an
accident. Anything which distracts us from driving,
either actively, like looking for a music cassette, or
passively, like daydreaming, reduces our control,
making an accident more likely.

Before you start your journey you should plan it to
minimise distraction. Estimate how long your journey
will take and plan:
• your route
• what to do at major junctions and intersections
• where you intend to take rest breaks.

Common distractions while driving

• *Conversation*.

• *Answering or making telephone calls*. If you need to
hold the receiver of your car telephone, you should
not use it while driving. Find somewhere safe to park
and then use the telephone. If you have a hands-free
car telephone, do not allow your conversation to
distract you from your driving. Again it is better to
find somewhere safe to stop before using the
telephone.

• *Using headphones*.

• *Looking at maps or guides*. You should plan your
route before you start.

• *Tuning the radio, or changing a cassette or CD*.

• *Excessively loud music*.

Even a moment's distraction could result in:
• driving off the road into pedestrians
• running into parked vehicles or the vehicle in front
• colliding with oncoming vehicles.

How to keep alert

Keeping up a good level of concentration can be
difficult, especially if driving conditions are
monotonous. The following advice will help to keep
you alert.

Sit comfortably

• Wear comfortable clothing, and shoes that give you good control of the pedals.

• Use whatever adjustments you have on your car (seat height, seat distance from wheel and pedals, angle of back rest, steering wheel adjustment) to adjust your seat so that you can reach and use the car controls easily.

• Adjust your seat belt so that it is comfortable and works correctly.

Get the interior conditions right

• Keep the car well ventilated, especially on long journeys.

• Get the temperature right: excessive warmth or coldness is tiring.

• Keep the noise levels down. High noise levels are tiring – keep your windows shut when travelling fast to avoid wind noise, and keep the stereo volume down.

See clearly

• Wear glasses if you need them.

• Keep glasses, mirrors and windows clean and smear-free.

• Adjust the mirrors so you can see through them comfortably.

• Remove any unnecessary stickers from the windows.
  Don't put anything in the windows which could
  obstruct your view.

IMPAIRMENT

An important part of keeping alert is avoiding those
things which impair alertness such as:
• poor eyesight
• tiredness
• distraction
• illness, medical conditions and medication
• alcohol/drugs
• anger and irritation.

Eyesight

To drive safely you need to be able to see properly.
The law sets a standard for your eyesight, which you
must reach whenever you drive.

• You must be able to read a vehicle number plate
  from a distance of 20.5 m (67 ft) at all times while
  driving. This is the standard required by the driving
  test. If you need glasses (or contact lenses) to be able
  to do this, you must wear them whenever you drive.

• When the sun is causing glare, position the visor
  carefully. Wearing sunglasses can help to reduce the
  strain on your eyes.

• Remember to remove your sunglasses if you enter a

low-light area such as a tunnel, multi-storey car park
or street shaded by tall buildings.

• Do not wear tinted glasses at night or in poor
  visibility because it will reduce your ability to see.

Tiredness

As you get tired, your ability to observe and make
decisions gets worse. If you continue to drive when
you are tired, you will eventually fall asleep and may
crash. Tiredness seriously threatens your life and the
lives of others.

• Long before you fall asleep you should recognise
  that you are tired and do something about it.

• The Highway Code says do not drive if you feel
  tired, and if you feel tired while driving, find a safe
  place to stop and rest.

Common causes of tiredness

• *Being tired before the journey starts.* If you drive
  when you would normally be asleep or after a day's
  work then you are more likely to suffer from
  tiredness during your journey. The time of greatest
  risk for fatigue-related accidents is between midnight
  and 8.00 am.

• *Long journeys*. The longer your journey the more
  likely you are to suffer from fatigue. On long
  journeys you need to take breaks at least every two
  hours: plan your rest breaks before you start.

- *Discomfort or excessive noise.* Adjust your seat so that you can reach the controls in comfort. Reduce noise wherever you can, for example by making sure that the windows are properly closed.

- *Insufficient ventilation.* Stuffy cars make you sleepy. Use the ventilators to ensure a fresh supply of air.

- *Boredom.* Driving in conditions which are monotonous causes fatigue. Examples of these conditions are long motorway journeys in light traffic, driving in fog or driving at night,

- *Poor visibility.* Driving at night or in other conditions of poor visibility – poor light, heavy rain, snow, fog – makes us tire more quickly. In these conditions take more rest breaks.

- *Age.* The older you are the more likely you are to suffer from fatigue. Drivers over 45 need to be particularly aware of this.

How to prevent tiredness

- Keep the car well ventilated.
- Take regular breaks from your driving – break for a minimum of 20 minutes every two hours of driving. Use the breaks to take some physical exercise, get refreshments or have a sleep.

If you feel tired while driving:

- make sure your car is well ventilated
- find somewhere safe to stop and take a rest
- until you can find somewhere safe to stop, drive more slowly to give yourself more time to react

Have some refreshment

- on a motorway, take the next exit and find somewhere safe to stop. It is illegal to stop on the hard shoulder of a motorway to take a rest. The hard shoulder is hazardous for you and other road users because of the risk of another vehicle running into you while you are stopped.

Take a nap

Illness, medical conditions and medication

Do not drive if:

- you feel unwell
- are ill
- are taking medicine which could affect your driving.

Some medicines can slow down your reactions.

• When you are prescribed a medicine always ask the doctor if it will affect your driving.

• If you take a non-prescribed medicine read the advice on the container and do not drive if it advises you not to.

• If you buy the medicine at a chemist's, the pharmacist will be able to tell you if it will affect your driving or not. If you are unsure about a medicine, ask your doctor. Until you have, do not drive.

Medicines which may affect your driving

Some, but not all, cough medicines can cause drowsiness so you must not drive when taking them. Read the advice on the container to find out if the particular medicine you are taking has this effect. Common prescription drugs which may affect your driving are sedatives and anti-depressants. If you take them, check with your doctor whether it is safe to drive.

WARNING: May cause drowsiness. If affected do not drive or operate machinery. Avoid alcoholic drink.

Medical conditions which may affect your driving

If you have a medical condition which affects your ability to drive you must not drive.

• If the condition is likely to last three months or more, you must notify the Driver and Vehicle Licensing Authority (DVLA) at Swansea.

• Your doctor will be able to advise you whether you have a condition that requires you to inform the DVLA.

• The driving licence application form lists the conditions that you must tell them about. If you do not tell the DVLA about a relevant illness or disability, your licence may not be valid.

Alcohol and drugs

The Road Traffic Act says that you must not drive under the influence of alcohol or drugs.

The affects of alcohol are serious:
• it markedly reduces your ability to drive
• it increases your confidence to drive at the same time.

The effect of alcohol, combining a decrease in actual driving ability with an increase in confidence, is lethal.

Alcohol contributes to more than 30% of all road accidents, and causes more than 500 road deaths a year.

Legal alcohol limits

The law sets a maximum level for the amount of
alcohol in your breath and in your blood. The levels
(which are equivalent) are:

• breath alcohol 35 µg/100 ml (35 micrograms per 100
  millilitres)

• blood alcohol 80 mg/100 ml (80 milligrams per 100
  millilitres)

Alcohol and driving

Alcohol affects your driving by:

• reducing coordination
• slowing your reactions
• affecting your judgement of
  – speed
  – distance
  – risk
• increasing your confidence.

Remember

• It is illegal to drive if you are above the legal limit.

• Being under the legal limit does not mean that you
  are necessarily safe to drive. Your driving might be
  seriously affected by your first drink.

• Half the alcohol from a drink enters your
  bloodstream within ten minutes. All the alcohol
  enters within an hour.

- Alcohol reacts with certain medicines, which on their own are perfectly safe, to seriously impair your driving.

- The only way to be sure that you are safe to drive is to follow the advice in the Highway Code – **do not drink and drive**.

Social events, driving and alcohol

- If you want to have a drink at a social event do not drive.

- If you drive to an event, and then decide to have a drink, arrange some other way of getting home first.

- Use public transport or arrange a lift with someone who is not going to drink if you intend to drink.

- Leave your car at home. The effects of alcohol make it more difficult to resist the temptation to drive once you have had a drink.

When are you safe to drive again after drinking?

- Your body gets rid of alcohol at a steady rate so the more you drink, the longer it takes your body to get rid of it.

- You may be unfit to drive in the evening if you have been drinking at lunchtime, or in the morning if you have been drinking the night before.

- Having a sleep, drinking a cup of strong coffee,

eating a meal or going for a walk does not remove
alcohol from your body any quicker.

• Time is the only thing that reduces the amount of
alcohol in your bloodstream. It could take 20 hours
to remove fully the alcohol in your bloodstream from
five or six pints of beer.

Drugs

Drugs impair your attention, perception of risk,
decision-making and speed of reaction. It is illegal to
drive under the influence of drugs.

Anger and irritation

Anger and irritation also impair your ability to drive.
This is covered in **2 Your attitude to driving**.

4 Recognising hazards

Increased risk for young drivers

Drivers under 25 are at a much higher risk of serious injury or death than more experienced drivers.

- Around one-sixth of all drivers are under 25.
- Half of all drivers killed or seriously injured are under 25.
- Per mile driven, a 17 year old man is seven times more likely to be involved in an accident than a middle-aged man.

RECOGNISING DANGER

The main explanation for this increased risk is inexperience. Young drivers are new drivers, and it is their failure to recognise and avoid danger that is the main cause of their accidents.

- In the first year of driving a 17 year old's risk of having an accident falls by 34%, but only 6% of the reduction is explained by their greater age.

Learning to recognise danger

Training in recognising hazards reduces the risk of having an accident. Finding out from experience that you should avoid braking on icy surfaces is a dangerous way to learn. Your first uncontrolled skid

39

might also be your last. It is clearly better to learn
about the risks through training rather than direct
experience.

In many respects, learning to drive is similar to
learning other skills.

• To perform a skilled activity we need to concentrate
  on what is relevant.

• Our ability to take in and process information is
  limited; we can only deal with a few bits of
  information at a time. We overcome this by sorting
  out the important bits of information and
  concentrating on them.

• Experience is the process of learning which are the
  important bits of information for the successful
  performance of the task.

• Inexperienced people either concentrate on the
  wrong information or fail to recognise what is
  important. This is where training can help.

The role of training

Training helps you to identify the information that is
critical for safe driving. This enables you to recognise
situations that may become hazardous. One reason
why older drivers are safer is that they recognise
hazardous situations early, thereby giving themselves
the time and the space to act. Younger, inexperienced
drivers have faster reactions, but sometimes do not
recognise when they are in danger until it is too late.

RECOGNISING AND DEALING WITH HAZARDS

A good driver:
• recognises hazards early
• assesses them
• takes action to deal with them before the situation
  gets worse.

Dealing with hazards

While you are driving you should bear in mind the
following six points for identifying and dealing with
hazards.

1 Be aware

Be aware of the likely hazards. Awareness enables
you to recognise and react to hazards before they
develop.

We see what we expect to see. In daylight collisions
between cars and motorcycles, one in three car
drivers fails to see the motorbike. This is not
because the bike isn't visible, but because the driver
wasn't sufficiently aware of motorbikes as potential
hazards, and was only looking for cars and lorries.

2 Observe

Observe the road carefully and continuously. Look
all around, to the far distance, the middle ground,
immediately in front, to the sides, and behind. Pay

attention to both what you can and cannot see. If
you cannot see the road ahead, slow down. Drive so
you can stop in the distance you can see to be clear.
Good observation is the key to safe driving.

3 Anticipate

Just looking is not sufficient. You have to interpret
what you see. Anticipate the hazards that could
develop from what you can see at the moment.
Anticipate unseen hazards. Anticipate the actions of
other road users. For example, if you see an ice-
cream van, you should anticipate children running
into the road without looking.

4 Assess

Assess the situation using the information available
to you, awareness (of possible hazards), and
anticipation (of what may happen next).

Anticipate unseen hazards

5 Decide

Having considered the options, decide on a course
and speed which removes or minimises the risks.

6 Act

When you have decided what to do, carry out your
actions calmly and efficiently.

At the end of this chapter there is a recommended
system for dealing with specific hazards known as
Mirror Signal Manoeuvre.

Observation

The better you observe, the more chance you have of
anticipating hazards. Make sure your observation
includes:

• other road users – who are they, what are they doing
• what is happening on the road ahead

- what sort of area you are in – town or country, residential, shopping or industrial
- what type of road is it, and whether there are any signs or road markings
- what the road conditions and surface conditions are like
- what the weather is like
- how your car is performing.

One way of improving your observation skills is by practising with someone who is more experienced. Next time you are a passenger with an experienced driver, look out for potential hazards and ask the driver to give you a running commentary on what they see and how they intend to respond to each hazard.

AWARENESS OF OTHER ROAD USERS

You need to be aware of the needs and vulnerabilities of other road users. An elderly pedestrian, a child cyclist or a large goods vehicle (LGV) use the road in different ways from a car driver.

- Elderly pedestrians are likely to react and move more slowly than younger people, and their eyesight and hearing are likely to be less good. They may not see you, or may underestimate your speed.
- Child cyclists are likely to wobble into your path, and as they gain in confidence they are likely to take horrifying risks.

• LGVs take relatively longer to stop, often straddle two lanes when turning left, are reluctant to lose speed going up hills and have restricted views to the side and rear.

Pedestrians in the road

Look out for pedestrians in the road at:
• traffic lights
• junctions
• pedestrian crossings
  – zebra crossings
  – pelican crossings
  – puffin crossings
  – school crossings
• shopping centres
• where there are crowds
• where there are no pavements.

Where you can see or expect pedestrians

• Drive slowly and be prepared to stop.

• Do not wave pedestrians across in front of you, because they might not check to see that they are safe from other vehicles.

• At junctions, give way to pedestrians who are already crossing the road.

• Give way to pedestrians on the pavement if you are using a driveway or entrance which crosses it.

• At pedestrian crossings, follow the instructions in the Highway Code.

You need to be aware of the times and places when other road users are likely to be about.

• If you are driving through the minor roads of a town or city, you should expect children to be around.

• When you are driving through a busy shopping centre, you should expect pedestrians to be standing in the road or crossing it.

• Between 8.00 and 9.00 am and again between 3.00 and 4.00 pm, you should expect schoolchildren to be around.

The whole point of being aware of other road users is to adapt your driving to minimise the risks associated with them.

• If you are driving through an area where there are likely to be children, reduce your speed so you could stop if a child ran out.

• Do not move up on the nearside of a lorry that starts to indicate left.

PARKED VEHICLES

Parked vehicles are a common feature of our roads, so it is important to understand and allow for the hazards associated with them. Parked vehicles are hazardous because:

• they restrict your vision

• they conceal pedestrians, especially children, right at the edge of your intended course

Parked vehicles may restrict your vision

- they restrict your view of other traffic, especially at junctions
- the occupants of parked vehicles may open doors or step out into your path
- vehicles may suddenly pull out from being parked, into your path.

The Highway Code additional information section, The theory of safe and responsible driving, recommends that in residential streets with parked cars you should normally drive not faster than 20 mph.

Where there are parked vehicles, drive slowly and be prepared to stop, position yourself as far away from the parked vehicles as you can without coming into conflict with oncoming vehicles.

Parked vehicles at junctions

Junctions are often obscured by parked vehicles.

• When you pull out of an obscured junction, stop at
  the edge of the road you are joining and move
  forward slowly until you can see whether it is safe to
  pull out fully.

• Always give way to traffic on the major road, and
  look carefully for cycles and motorcycles.

• If you are on the major road, anticipate junctions by
  gaps in the rows of parked vehicles. If it is safe,
  position your vehicle more to the offside, so you can
  see into the junction. Restrict your speed so you
  could stop if a vehicle suddenly pulled out of the
  junction.

Space and speed

Parked vehicles illustrate a general safety principle:
the trade off between space and speed.

• The space around your vehicle is your safety margin.

• The bigger the space around you, the more you can
  see and the longer you have to react.

• When space is restricted, you must reduce your
  speed to give yourself more time to react.

Where you can't move away from parked vehicles,
you need to restrict your speed so that you could stop
if a child jumped out of the next gap.

Parked vehicles summary

Parked cars are one of the hazards to which drivers
have to adapt. You must adapt your driving to their
presence and deal with them with flexibility and
patience.

When you see a line of cars parked along the road
ahead think:
• pedestrians, especially children
• opening car doors
• vehicles pulling out
• concealed junctions.

STOPPING DISTANCES

You must know how long it will take your vehicle to
stop at different speeds and in different conditions.
You need to know the shortest stopping distances for
your own safety and for the theory test. For the theory
test you will need to remember these distances in
metres (or feet) and in car lengths. Shortest stopping
distances in car lengths are given on the back cover of
the Highway Code.

The shortest stopping distances

• The shortest stopping distances give the shortest
  distance in which you can stop at different speeds,
  in good conditions. When the road is slippery
  because of rain, snow or ice, it will take longer to
  stop.

- The stopping distance is made up of two parts: thinking distance and braking distance.

- **Thinking distance** gives the distance your vehicle will travel between recognising that you need to brake and actually starting to brake. If you are tired or unwell you will travel further because your reactions will be slower.

- **Braking distance** is the shortest distance it will take to stop once you start braking. This is the distance *in good conditions*. If the roads are slippery it will take longer.

The shortest stopping distance is given by adding thinking distance to braking distance.

**Shortest stopping distance
= thinking distance + braking distance.**

Speed in mph	Thinking distance in metres	Braking distance in metres	Stopping distance in metres	Stopping distance in car lengths
20	6	6	12	3
30	9	14	23	6
40	12	24	36	9
50	15	38	53	13
60	18	55	73	18
70	21	75	96	24

For Highway Code purposes, a car length is four metres, so if you know the stopping distance in metres you can work out the stopping distance in car lengths by dividing by four.

At 20 mph in dry conditions *your stopping distance is*
3 car lengths

At 30 mph in dry conditions *your stopping distance is*
6 car lengths

At 20 mph in wet conditions *your stopping distance is*
12 car lengths

At 20mph in icy conditions *your stopping distance is*
30 car lengths

Using shortest stopping distances

- You should always be able to stop in the distance
  you can see to be clear. The shortest stopping
  distances give you a guide to the maximum speed for
  the distance you can see ahead.

- If, for example, you can see only six car lengths
  ahead, then you should not go faster than 30 mph,
  because six car lengths is the minimum distance in
  which you could stop at 30 mph.

These are the shortest stopping distances in good conditions only.

• In wet conditions stopping distances can be up to four times as long.

• In icy conditions they can be up to ten times as long.

Note that if you double your speed you double your thinking distance, but quadruple your braking distance. Stopping distances increase disproportionately with speed. Adapting your speed to the circumstances is essential for road safety.

FOLLOWING DISTANCES

Learning to recognise and avoid hazards is the key to safe driving. Excessive speed and following too closely are major causes of accidents.

• Drivers who speed have higher than average accident risk.

• Following too closely accounts for one in three of all accidents.

The advice in the *Key principles for safe driving* is 'always be able to stop in the distance you can see to be clear'. This advice sets the safe speed for all driving circumstances except single track roads. On these you need to be able to stop in less than half the distance that you can see to be clear. This allows oncoming vehicles sufficient space to stop in also.

Controlling the distance between yourself and the vehicle in front is one of the most effective ways you have to protect yourself.

• The greater the following distance the more time you have to stop.

• The distance between your vehicle and the vehicle in front affects the likelihood of the vehicle behind running into you. The greater your distance from the vehicle in front, the more gently you can brake, thereby giving the vehicle behind more time and space to stop also.

Safe following distances

Safe following distances from the vehicle in front depend on:

• your level of attention
• your speed
• the condition of the road surface.

• If your attention is not at its best, you need to allow more space to give yourself sufficient time to react.

• The faster you go, the further you will travel before you react, and the longer it will take you to stop.

• The more slippery the road surface, the poorer your tyre grip and the greater the distance it will take you to stop.

What distances should you allow?

• As a safe rule for following the vehicle in front, the Highway Code recommends that you should not get closer than the safe stopping distances given in the table on page 50.

• This separation distance is not always possible so the Driving Standards Agency say that a reasonable separation in good conditions is one metre per mile per hour between you and the vehicle in front. So at 55 mph there should be a 55-metre gap between you and the vehicle in front (equivalent to nearly 14 car lengths).

If you follow too close behind a large vehicle, your view will be restricted.

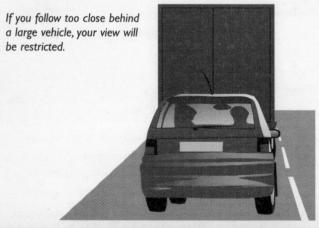

- In good conditions on a road carrying fast traffic, the Highway Code says a two-second gap between you and the vehicle in front may be sufficient. What is meant by a two-second gap is explained below.

Variations for different conditions

- In wet conditions stopping distances can be up to four times longer, so increase your following distance by a corresponding amount.

- In icy conditions stopping distances can be up to ten times greater, so you need to increase your following distance by a corresponding amount.

- In slow-moving traffic it may not be possible to follow the advice of one metre per mile per hour, nor

Drop back so that you can get a better view.

even of a two-second gap. However, you must
always keep a sufficient distance in which to stop if
the vehicle in front brakes or changes direction.

When you stop, you should always allow a sufficient
gap for you to be able to pull round the vehicle in
front if it becomes necessary. A good guide to this
distance, for car drivers, is to stay sufficiently behind
the vehicle in front to be able to see its rear tyres from
the normal driving position.

The two-second rule

In good conditions and in fast traffic, you should leave
at least a two-second gap between yourself and the
vehicle in front. To work out this gap:

• choose a feature on the side of the road such as a
  lamp-post or street sign to act as a marker

• count off the seconds between the vehicle in front
  passing the marker and when you pass it

• if the gap is less than two seconds, drop back from
  the vehicle in front until it is at least two seconds.

A convenient way of calculating two seconds is to
say to yourself *'Only a fool breaks the two-second
rule'*.

If you can't say all of this before you pass the
marker, drop back until you can. In wet conditions
this time gap should be at least doubled to four
seconds because of the reduced grip of the tyres on
the road.

MIRROR SIGNAL MANOEUVRE

Whatever road you are on you will have to deal with hazards.

- A hazard is anything which is potentially dangerous. Examples are junctions, roundabouts, blind bends, other road users, overtaking, slippery roads – any object, activity or situation that bears an element of risk.
- The way to cope with hazards is by controlling your position and speed.
- The Highway Code has a standardised procedure for doing this. It is known by the names or the initials of the different stages: **Mirror Signal Manoeuvre – Position Speed Look**, or **MSM PSL**.

Mirrors

Before you change position or speed, check your mirrors so you know what is happening all around you.

Signal

If a signal would benefit other road users, including pedestrians, give it before you start to manoeuvre.

Manoeuvre

Make the manoeuvre, if it is safe, keeping up your observation all the time. Use the PSL routine to make the manoeuvre.

Position

Try to get into position for the manoeuvre early. It
helps other road users recognise what you are
doing.

Speed

Get the right speed for the manoeuvre. If this
involves slowing down or stopping, check your
mirrors first.

Look

Keep up all-round observation (including mirrors)
throughout your manoeuvre, and especially before
you turn or move into another lane. You should
know from your observation that the space you
intend to turn into is free from approaching
vehicles, either from in front or from behind.

Use MSM PSL during the approach and negotiation of
hazards. Used systematically:
• it helps you to anticipate the problems associated
  with different hazards
• gives you the time to deal with them calmly
• helps you to drive in a controlled and thoughtful
  way.

5 Vulnerable road users

PEDESTRIANS

In built-up areas, you should expect pedestrians to be about. Look to see where they are, and drive slowly.

> If you are driving at 40 mph and you hit someone, you will probably kill them. At 20 mph, 19 out of 20 people will survive the accident.

Wherever you are, look for pedestrians. If they are present, reduce your speed. The pedestrian checklist below identifies areas where you should be particularly watchful.

Pedestrian checklist

Is it an area where pedestrians are likely?
• built-up areas
• villages and hamlets
• shopping centres
• national parks
• local beauty spots

Are there likely to be pedestrians from high-risk groups?
• children
• elderly people

- partially sighted people (identifiable by their white sticks or guide dogs)
- hearing impaired people
- revellers

Are pedestrians likely to be in the road?
- no pavements
- pedestrian crossings
- junctions
- service vehicles
- residential areas
- roadside buildings and amenities

Are there any service vehicles which pedestrians might be crossing to or returning from?
- ice-cream vans, hot-dog vans
- buses, coaches, taxis and trams
- mobile grocers, milk floats

Are there any roadside buildings or amenities which pedestrians might be crossing to or returning from?
- shops and takeaways
- playgrounds and parks
- schools, colleges, hospitals, nursing homes, residential homes
- stadiums
- pubs, cinemas, theatres, bingo halls and clubs

Is there anything which restricts your view of the pavement or road, and from behind which a pedestrian could step out?

• parked or halted vehicles
• slow-moving or halted vehicles, especially tall vehicles (off roaders, buses, vans and lorries)
• kiosks, road works, buildings and walls
• vegetation
• sharp bends

Where there are pedestrians, think about your position and speed. Position your car to give pedestrians extra space if you can (without getting in the way of oncoming vehicles), and reduce your speed to one that is consistent with the risks.

Be aware of children concealed by parked vehicles

CHILDREN

When children are around you have to take particular
care. Children:

• don't understand the risks posed by traffic

• are not experienced at judging speed and distance

• forget to check before crossing roads

• do not have the same automatic response to road
  safety as adults

• are small and often difficult to see. They may be
  concealed by the bodywork of your car or may be
  concealed behind parked vehicles.

Children get easily excited, and in the pursuit of the
moment may completely ignore road safety. You
cannot rely on their own sense of self-preservation to
protect them.

Children – ice-cream vans and balls

Anything that attracts a child is likely to make them
forget about the traffic.

• If that person, animal or thing is in the road, or on
  the other side of the road, children are likely to run
  to and from it.

• Children run into the road without a thought after
  balls, balloons, animals, each other and ice-cream
  vans.

• If you see a child running, walking with a dog off its

lead or playing with a ball, reduce your speed and
take extra care.

• You have to think safety for children – slow down
  and be prepared to stop.

Once children are frightened, they may react
unpredictably. They may ignore horn warnings and
light flashes, and are just as likely to run into danger
as away from it.

Dealing with ice-cream vans

• When you see an ice-cream van, look for children on
  both sides of the road and reduce your speed.

• If there are parked vehicles, anticipate the possibility
  of children dashing out from between them, or from
  behind the van.

• As you move out to pass the van, slow right down. If
  oncoming traffic means that you would have to pass
  close to the van, stop and wait until there is no
  oncoming traffic.

• Equalise the space between yourself and the van on
  the one side and yourself and the parked cars on the
  other.

• The less space between yourself, and the vehicles on
  each side, the slower you must go

• Remember, even at 20 mph, it takes three car lengths
  to stop.

SCHOOLCHILDREN

When you drive through residential areas or villages, you should be on the look-out for schoolchildren, especially at the beginning and end of the school day, and during the lunch break. In your own area, you probably know where the schools are, but outside your area you will have to rely on your observations and road signs to identify them.

• It is important to know that you are approaching a school because children are likely to be crowding on the pavements, spilling into the road and crossing the road.

• On the approach to schools, the Highway Code says you should drive very slowly until you are well clear of the area.

• Look for the 'school bus' sign displayed in the front or rear windows of buses. See **Vehicle Markings** in the Highway Code.

• If a school bus is stopped, pass it slowly and give it a wide berth – children may run across to it or dash from behind it.

• Do not stop on the yellow lined area outside a school marked SCHOOL KEEP CLEAR, even to drop off or pick up children. The purpose of the area is to provide clear sightlines for both schoolchildren and drivers.

The school warning sign

The basic road sign for a school is a
triangular warning sign showing
two children running. See the
Highway Code **Warning Signs**
for an illustration of the sign.
Underneath the sign there
are different qualifying
plates:

Words on plate	Meaning
School	School children nearby
Playground	Playground ahead
Disabled children Blind children Deaf children	Children with the specified disability nearby
Patrol	School crossing patrol ahead

• In addition to the school warning sign there may be
  amber warning lights, mounted one above the other
  on an upright black plate. These flash when children
  are likely to be crossing the road.

School crossing patrols

• Look up the 'school crossing patrol' sign in the
  Highway Code section, **Signs giving orders**.

- School crossing patrols (lollipop ladies and men) help children to cross the road in safety.

- You must not pass a crossing patrol sign if it is displayed by the crossing patrol.

- When a school crossing patrol sign is displayed, stop and wait for the children to cross. Do not move forward until the attendant withdraws the sign.

- Expect to see patrols on busy streets near to or on the approach to schools.

When you see flashing amber lights on the approach to a school:

- slow down and anticipate children in the road
- look for children on the pavement and in the road, anticipate their movements
- look for school buses and anticipate children in the road around them
- look for a school crossing patrol
- look for the school.

ELDERLY PEOPLE

Elderly people may have reduced vision or hearing. They may not be aware of your presence or they may miscalculate your speed and distance. They may have mobility difficulties so that it takes them longer to cross the road. When you see elderly people on the kerbside or in the road:

- slow down

• position yourself away from them if you can do so
  safely
• give them the time that they need to cross the road.

PEDESTRIANS WITH SIGHT OR HEARING IMPAIRMENT

Pedestrians of any age could have sight or hearing
impairment, so do not assume that pedestrians can see
or hear you until they react to your presence.

• Blind or partially sighted people may require longer
  to cross the road and may hesitate at junctions or
  crossings. Be patient and give them time.

• People with hearing difficulties may be unaware of
  your presence and may not hear horn warnings.
  When you use your horn, use it in good time and
  look to see if the person reacts.

• The disabled children warning sign warns of areas
  where there are likely to be blind or deaf children.

• The 'elderly people' warning sign warns where
  elderly, blind or disabled people may be crossing the
  road. See the Highway Code, **Warning signs** for an
  illustration of the elderly people sign.

White sticks and guide dogs

While you are driving, you should be continually
scanning the pavement, as well as the road, for
information.

- If you see a person with a white stick or a guide dog, it means that the person is blind or partially sighted.

- If the stick has two red reflective bands it means that the carrier is deaf and blind. Use this information to plan your driving.

- Do not expect a person with a white stick or guide dog to be fully aware of your presence. Position away from them, reduce your speed and, if they look like they might step into the road, be prepared to stop.

PEDESTRIANS IN THE ROAD

Pedestrians in the road are an obvious hazard. Look out for them at traffic lights, junctions, pedestrian crossings, shopping centres, where there are crowds and where there are no pavements. Where there are pedestrians in the road:

- drive slowly and be prepared to stop

- at junctions, give way to pedestrians who are already crossing the road

- give way to pedestrians on the pavement if you are using a driveway or entrance which crosses it

- never wave pedestrians across in front of you – it might cause them to ignore the threat from other vehicles.

No footpaths

Where there are no footpaths, expect pedestrians to be in the road.

• This is most common in country districts, where you should normally expect pedestrians walking towards you to be on your side of the road. Or at least the Highway Code advises pedestrians to walk facing the traffic.

• In fact, near to beauty spots, popular public footpaths and on bends, pedestrians may well be on either side of the road and walking in either direction.

• In built-up areas, you are more likely to see a 'pedestrians in road ahead' warning sign, where there is no footpath. See the illustration of this sign in the Highway Code, **Warning signs** section.

PEDESTRIANS AT JUNCTIONS

The Highway Code advises you to take extra care at junctions. This is because road users move across each other's paths and visibility is often reduced by buildings, vegetation, traffic and parked vehicles.

• The Highway Code says that pedestrians, cyclists and motorcyclists are at particular risk at junctions.

• Pedestrians have to cross the road at junctions. They are at risk both from vehicles turning into the junction and from vehicles pulling out of it. Also pedestrians often cross between vehicles queuing to

pull out of a junction, so take care as you edge
forward.

- If you are turning into a junction, you must give way
  to pedestrians crossing it. The Highway Code is quite
  explicit on this point. Pedestrians have priority whether
  you drive forwards into the junction or reverse into it.
  If you are reversing into a junction, you need to take
  extra care to make sure there are no pedestrians,
  especially children, immediately behind you, or
  crossing the junction.

Before you turn into a junction, **look for pedestrians
crossing or about to cross. If there are any, give way
to them. If your view into the junction is restricted
by buildings or parked vehicles, slow right down.**

Before moving out of a junction, **make sure that
there are no pedestrians standing in front of your
vehicle, or crossing your intended path.**

PEDESTRIANS AND BUSES

Pedestrians step from behind buses and cross the road
to and from them.

- When you approach a stopped bus, whichever side
  of the road it is on, expect pedestrians in the road.
- Look for pedestrians, slow down and position
  yourself well away from the bus when you pass it.
- If you cannot give the bus a wide berth, go even
  slower.

CYCLISTS

Cyclists are another highly vulnerable group of road users. Like pedestrians and motorcyclists they do not have a steel shell to protect them. Unlike pedestrians, their normal place is in the road, sharing the space with fast-moving lumps of steel.

• When you see a cyclist think of their vulnerability.

• Cycles are relatively unstable. Winds, potholes, uneven road surfaces, opening car doors and steep gradients can easily cause cyclists to swerve off course and into your path.

• Cyclists' brakes are relatively inefficient, their lights are weak, and they have to remove a hand from the handlebars to signal.

• Always give cyclists plenty of space when you are following them.

• When you overtake cyclists, give them the same space as you would for a car.

• Remember that cyclists may be slow, and that at junctions they may take any course. Cyclists are not very visible and are particularly vulnerable at junctions because drivers fail to see them.

• At roundabouts cyclists may occupy the nearside lane all the way round, so be careful not to cut across them at exits.

• If you see a cyclist in an unexpected place, be cautious: they might *do* something unexpected also.

Position your car away from them to give them extra
space, and reduce your speed to give them extra
time.

Cyclists and left-hand turns

• Never attempt to overtake a cyclist just before you
make a left-hand turn.

• If a cyclist is in front, follow at a safe distance
behind the cyclist. Turn into the junction after the
cyclist has passed.

• In slow-moving traffic, always check before making
a left-hand turn that no cyclists have moved up on
your nearside. If they have, let them pass before
turning.

Cyclists and roundabouts

• Cyclists may approach a roundabout in the left lane,
and keep to the left lane round the roundabout,
whatever exit they intend to take.

• Take care not to cut across cyclists if you leave the
roundabout before them.

• Cyclists may also follow the standard approaches
and routes on roundabouts.

• Remember that they are slower, and give them plenty
of space.

Overtaking cyclists

- Before you overtake a cyclist, look ahead to see if there are any hazards that might make the cyclist change course.

- Cyclists often swerve suddenly to avoid hazards such as open car doors and potholes. They wobble under their rider's exertions, and are easily blown off course by the wind.

- If the way looks clear, give the cyclist as much room as you would for a car. On windy days give them more room.

Give a cyclist as much room as you would a car when overtaking

CYCLISTS AND MOTORCYCLISTS AT JUNCTIONS

Cyclists and motorcyclists are at particular risk from vehicles colliding with them at junctions.

• About one-third of drivers who knock over motorcyclists say that they did not see the machine.

• Research shows that drivers allow less room when pulling out in front of an approaching motorcycle than they do for a car or lorry.

Visibility

Cycles and motorbikes are:

• smaller than other vehicles, and therefore less easy to see

• easily concealed by other vehicles

• narrow in outline, making it difficult to assess their speed

• not seen by drivers, because drivers do not expect to see them.

As a driver, you have to train yourself to look for cyclists and motorcyclists when:

• pulling out at a junction

• turning right into a junction

• turning left into a junction.

You also have to allow greater safety margins when assessing their speed of approach.

At junctions, look for cyclists and motorcyclists. Allow them a greater safety margin. Don't pull across them.

This really is important advice. Motorcyclists are 35 times more likely to be killed or seriously injured than drivers.

MOTORCYCLES

Motorcyclists have very similar needs and vulnerabilities as cyclists, but because they go faster, the results of any miscalculations or failures to see by you are likely to be much more devastating.

- At junctions look carefully for motorcyles before pulling out.
- Before turning right, look carefully (back and front) for motorcycles.
- Before pulling out to overtake, look carefully (back and front) for motorcycles.
- When overtaking motorcycles, give them as much room as you would for a car.
- Allow motorcycles much more room on windy days.
- Expect motorcycles to swerve out as they pull clear of the side-suction of a fast-moving lorry.
- On wet days give motorcycles more space – road markings, metal covers and tar bands round road repairs become very slippery for motorcycles.

HORSES AND OTHER ANIMALS

Horses and other animals are easily startled by noise, speed and vehicles which are too close. So when you encounter animals in the road:

• Follow them slowly, at a good distance, and be ready to stop.

• Do not rev your engine or sound your horn because this may startle the animals.

• When you overtake, drive slowly and keep well away from them.

Horses

• Horse riders generally keep to the left side of the road, and may not move to the centre of the road before turning right.

• On roundabouts, horse riders may keep to the left on the approach and while they are going round the roundabout, whichever exit they intend to take. Watch for their signals as to their intended course. They should give a right arm signal if they do not intend to take the next exit.

• On left-hand bends, horse riders are difficult to see. So if you are somewhere where you might expect horse riders, reduce your speed on the approach to left-hand bends and, if safe, position your car towards the centre of your side of the road to get a better view.

• If you see horse riders ahead slow down. If the horse riders appear to be a group from a riding school, take extra care because there may be learner riders in the group.

Overtaking horse riders

If you see horse riders ahead and you want to overtake them:

• check your mirror, slow down smoothly, and be prepared to stop
• take up a following position well back from the riders
• when an overtaking opportunity arises, move well out from the horses and overtake at a steady pace
• avoid making any unnecessary noise.

Livestock

• In the country, you should expect animals to be in the road.
• There may be signs warning of cattle, sheep or accompanied horses. See the illustration in the Highway Code, **Warning signs**.
• Flashing amber lights above a cattle warning sign indicate a supervised cattle crossing ahead.
• Where there are warning signs, look ahead for the animals, reduce your speed and prepare to stop.

DRIVERS AT RISK

Driver error plays a part in 95% of all accidents. By contrast, mechanical defects and road design are responsible for less than 5% of all accidents. The toll of these accidents in death and suffering is dreadful. Each day, about ten people are killed, 125 are seriously injured and 725 are slightly injured on our roads.

High-risk groups

• Not all drivers are equally likely to have an accident.

• You are most likely to have an accident in your first year of driving.

• As you develop experience and understanding of the risks involved, you become a safer driver.

• The group most likely to be involved in an accident is 17 to 25 year olds.

The main explanation for this greater risk is inexperience rather than age.

Gender

• Besides age, the other main indicator of accident risk is sex.

• On average, young men are twice as likely to have a fatal accident as young women.

• This changes with age – middle-aged men have similar accident rates to middle-aged women.

It is important to recognise that you can do something about your accident risk if you are in a high-risk category. By adopting different attitudes to risk and aggression, and by training in hazard perception and driving skills, you can significantly alter your risks.

Elderly drivers

Elderly drivers are likely to have slower reactions. Be patient, and give them extra time and space.

MOTORWAY DRIVING

Per mile travelled, motorways are safer than roads, but because of the speed at which vehicles travel any misjudgements or mistakes can have serious consequences.

• You are strongly advised by the Driving Standards Agency to take practical training in motorway driving.

• You will not receive practical training on motorways while preparing for your practical driving test, because learner drivers are not permitted on motorways.

• Instruction on dual carraigeways provides some experience, but the best way to train is to take specific motorway instruction after you have passed the test.

• Schemes such as the Pass Plus scheme, delivered by approved driving instructors, provide this instruction.

6 Different types of road

This chapter looks at the broad differences between roads and deals with motorways in detail. Detailed regulations governing roads other than motorways are covered in the chapters on **Crossings, junctions and roundabouts**, **Rules of the road** and **Signs and signals**.

The types of road covered are:
- single-track roads
- single carriageways
- one-way streets
- dual carriageways
- motorways

SINGLE-TRACK ROADS

Single-track roads are roads that are only wide enough for a single vehicle. In towns there are often short sections of single-track road; in the countryside you may encounter fairly long sections.

- They may have passing-places, which are like small lay-bys, to enable vehicles to pass each other.
- If you see another vehicle approaching, pull into a passing-place if there is one on your side of the road.
- If the passing-place is on the opposite side of the

road, stop opposite it, so that the other vehicle can
pull in when it reaches you.

- If you are travelling slowly, pull into passing-places
  on the left of the road to allow vehicles behind to
  overtake.

- Do not park in passing-places.

- Give way to vehicles coming uphill on single-track
  roads.

- When someone gives way to you, remember the
  importance of courtesy, and thank them.

- On single-track roads, travel at a speed that allows
  you to stop in half the distance that you can see to be
  clear. This gives oncoming vehicles sufficient space
  to stop also.

SINGLE CARRIAGEWAYS

- Single carriageways have traffic travelling in both
  directions, so always be aware of the hazards posed
  by oncoming traffic. Take great care when overtaking
  on single carriageways.

- There may be two, three or more lanes; the lane
  markings will tell you which lanes you can use to
  travel in your direction. Where there are four or more
  lanes, do not use the lanes on the right unless signs
  and road markings say you can.

- Where a single carriageway has three lanes and the

middle lane may be used by traffic travelling in
either direction, use only the middle lane for
overtaking. Take great care in using it: oncoming
traffic has just as much right to use it as you. Do not
use the right lane.

Side roads

• Where side roads join on to a major road, you should
look carefully for vehicles pulling out in front of
you, on to the major road.

• As in any other hazardous situation, consider your
position and speed and be prepared to stop if
necessary.

ONE-WAY STREETS

One-way streets are streets along which you can travel
in one direction only. They are identified by street
signs. See the Highway Code, **Traffic signs** for the
relevant signs. Note the different meanings of the
rectangular blue sign with a white arrow and the
circular blue sign with a white arrow.

• In one-way streets you may overtake in any lane, so
expect vehicles to pass on either side of you.

• In one-way streets, move into the appropriate lane
for your exit in plenty of time, so that you don't
disrupt other road users when you leave.

DUAL CARRIAGEWAYS

On dual carriageways, traffic travelling in different directions is separated by a central reservation. Each carriageway of a dual carriageway is usually at least two lanes wide. On dual carriageways:

• use only the right lane for overtaking or turning right

• where there are more than two lanes, move into a lane to the right only to overtake a vehicle in your present lane. When you are not overtaking and it is safe to do so, return to the leftmost lane.

Road works on dual carriageways

Lanes or whole carriageways may be closed for road works. Signs are provided to give advance warning of road works and to give directions on lane use. You must obey any temporary speed limit signs. The normal sequence of signing before road works is:

2 miles	advance warning of type of road works
1 mile	advance warning of road works and delays
¾ mile	warning of a mandatory (compulsory) temporary speed limit ahead
800 yards 400 yards 200 yards	signs showing which lanes are closed and the course to take through the road works

There are many variations on road works signs. See the Highway Code, **Traffic signs** for illustrations of the main types of sign. The key signs are signs which show:

• temporary mandatory speed limits
• lane closures
• lane diversions and contraflows
• the end of the road works.

Temporary lane closure The black arrows show the position and number of lanes that are open; the red bars show the position and number of lanes that are closed. They are both varied according to the circumstances.

One lane crossover at contraflow The black arrows show the number and direction of lane changes. The black bar between the arrowheads represents the central reservation. The right-hand lane crosses over the central reservation on to the other carriageway. Arrows and directions are varied according to circumstances.

End of road works and any temporary restrictions

A contraflow is where traffic travelling in opposite directions temporarily shares the same carriageway. Contraflows are hazardous.

• The lanes may be narrow.

• Traffic is travelling in opposite directions close to each other.

• You are twice as likely to have an accident in contraflows.

In contraflows, follow the advised speed limit and keep a good distance between you and the vehicle in front.

Road works temporary mandatory speed limit sign

This sign is not illustrated in the Highway Code. You must comply with its speed limit. It is illustrated here.

Road works temporary mandatory speed limit

MOTORWAYS

It is against the law to drive on a motorway until you have passed your test. So you will not be able to use some of the following information until you have got a full driving certificate. However, much of the information is also applicable to driving on dual carriageways and other roads.

Motorways and safety

• Per mile travelled, motorways are the safest roads but, because of the speeds, if anything does go wrong they can be very dangerous.

• If you make an error of judgement or overlook some crucial piece of information you could have a serious accident.

• The speed and volume of traffic on motorways makes it essential that you know exactly what you are doing when you drive on motorways.

• You are strongly recommended to take training in motorway driving after you pass your test. Schemes such as PASS PLUS are widely available and are designed to develop your motorway driving skills.

Who must not use a motorway

Motorways must not be used by:
• provisional licence holders
• pedestrians
• cyclists
• horse riders
• motorcycles under 50 cc
• certain slow-moving vehicles
• agricultural vehicles such as tractors
• invalid carriages weighing 254 kg and under
• animals.

Slow-moving vehicles carrying oversized loads may use the motorway by special permission.

Preparing for a motorway journey

Before you use a motorway you need to be adequately prepared.

• You need to be alert and free from any of the impairments discussed in **3 Alertness and impairment**.

• Your vehicle needs to be in a roadworthy condition. Long high-speed journeys put your vehicle under stress. Carry out a POWER check (see **8 Vehicle safety**) before starting your journey.

• Any loads you are carrying or pulling need to be in a fit condition and adequately secured.

• Avoid running out of fuel on the motorway. It is dangerous to lose power when you and the surrounding traffic are travelling at speed. It is also dangerous waiting for help on the hard shoulder.

• Remember to take a break at least every two hours.

• Plan your route. Before you start your journey, plan which exit you are going to take and what you are going to do at any intersections on your route.

• Know the rules in the **Motorways** section of the Highway Code before driving on the motorway and follow them.

You must not reverse or do a U-turn on a motorway. You may only stop on the hard shoulder of a motorway in an emergency.

Joining the motorway

Motorways are joined using a slip road, which merges
at an angle with the motorway. Slip roads enable you
to build up speed and observe the traffic already on
the motorway.

• Use the slip road to build up your speed to match
  that of traffic already on the motorway, and to look
  for a safe gap in the motorway traffic into which you
  can slot.

• Try to adjust your speed so that you merge smoothly
  into the motorway traffic, without having to stop.

• If you cannot merge smoothly you must stop. You
  must give way to traffic already on the motorway.

Speed limits on motorways

The national speed limit on motorways depends on the
type of vehicle you are driving. In this book we
consider only the national speed limit as it applies to
cars and motorcycles and cars towing caravans or
trailers. Additional speed limit signs may reduce the
speed limit on particular stretches of motorway.

National speed limits on motorways

Cars, motorcycles and car-derived vans	70 mph
Cars towing caravans or trailers	60 mph

- Remember these are the maximum speed limits. When the road is slippery or the visibility is low or the traffic is very dense these may be much too fast for safety. Always adjust your speed to the conditions.

- Vehicles pulling a trailer must not use the right-hand lane on motorways with three or more lanes. This also applies to cars towing a caravan.

- Vehicles with trailers and large goods vehicles must not use the right-hand lane on motorways with three or more lanes. If you are in the middle lane and one of these vehicles wants to overtake, move out of its way if it is safe to do so.

- Where there are road works or poor visibility or some other disruption to the traffic flow, the matrix signs on the side of the motorway or on the gantries overhead may advise a lower maximum speed. Follow this advice even if you cannot immediately see what the problem is. At the moment the speed limits on these signs are advisory; they may well be made mandatory in the future.

- Temporary maximum speed signs at road works are mandatory and you must obey them. The temporary mandatory speed limit is shown as the familiar black number on a white background, ringed in red, but it is placed on a yellow rectangular board. The board may carry other information as well.

Lane use and overtaking on motorways

The lanes on a motorway are identified as in the illustration below:

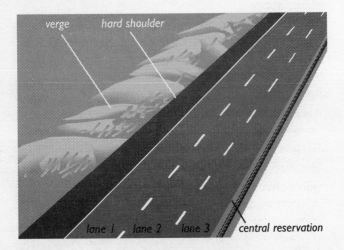

The lanes are numbered upwards from lane 1, which is the lane nearest the hard shoulder, as far as the central reservation. Each carriageway is numbered separately.

- Keep to the left except when overtaking.

- When you have finished overtaking, return to the left when it is safe to do so.

- Apart from specifically designated crawler lanes, there are no slow or fast lanes on motorways.

- Lane 1 is for use by all vehicles at all speeds. The lanes to the right are for overtaking.

Overtaking on motorways

• Before overtaking on a motorway, check your
mirrors and make sure you know what is in your
blind spot.

• Do not pull out to overtake if you would force a
vehicle behind to change its direction or speed.

• Do not start indicating until there is a clear space in
the lane to your right to pull into.

• When you plan to overtake, indicate first, then start
to move position. Do not indicate and move position
simultaneously.

• Watch carefully for a slower-moving vehicle in front
suddenly pulling out.

• Give yourself plenty of room to move out smoothly,
and similarly give yourself plenty of room when you
return. Avoid sudden jerky movements.

• Remember the two-second rule (see page 56).

Overtaking on the left or on the hard shoulder

• Do not overtake to the left of slower-moving
vehicles, except when traffic is moving in queues
and the queue on your right is moving more slowly
than you are.

• Do not move into a lane on your left to overtake.

• Never use the hard shoulder for overtaking, unless
your lane of traffic has been diverted on to the hard
shoulder, is moving in queues and the queue to your
right is moving more slowly than you are.

Motorways at night

• You must always use your headlights on motorways at night, even if the road is well lit.

• Dip your headlights if you are following other vehicles so that the light from your beam falls short of them.

• Only switch off your headlights on a motorway if you have had to stop on the hard shoulder because of an emergency. Leave your sidelights on, and switch on your hazard warning lights. If possible, get everyone out of the car and on to the verge. Phone the emergency services and go back to wait near the car but on the verge away from danger.

Reflective studs on motorways

Lanes are marked out by coloured reflective studs (Catseyes) and white paint markings. The colour of the studs varies according to which part of the motorway you are on.

• Red studs mark the left edge of the carriageway (between lane 1 and the hard shoulder).

• Green studs mark slip road entrances and exits.

• Amber studs mark the right edge of the carriageway, next to the central reservation.

• White studs mark the boundaries between lanes.

Road works on motorways

Road works are a common feature on motorways because of the need for continual maintenance. Generally the motorway is kept open, which means that the traffic has to be diverted on to fewer lanes. This causes hold-ups and sharp increases in the density of traffic. Tempers get frayed and drivers drive too close to each other. The risk of an accident in contraflows is about twice the normal rate. The way to avoid accidents is to:

• be patient
• keep a good distance between yourself and the vehicle in front
• keep to temporary speed limits
• comply with advice about lane use
• keep to your lane and not try to jump queues
• show restraint and not try to prevent other drivers from jumping queues.

Lane closures and diversions

• Where road works signs advise you that your lane is closed ahead, move over into another lane as soon as it is safe to do so. See rules 170 to 173 of the Highway code and the section on **Light signals controlling lights**.

• If your lane is to remain open but other lanes are to close, allow vehicles from other lanes to merge into yours. The routing signs may direct traffic to use the hard shoulder. Follow the directions.

- Lanes through road works are often narrower than normal lanes, so take care and keep your speed down.

- It is important to get your speed down before you enter a contraflow because the entry is often a fairly sharp S-bend, and the road surface fairly uneven. If you are going too fast you may lose control of the car.

Motorway signals

- Motorway signals are placed on the central reservation, on gantries over the motorway, and at the back of the hard shoulder.

- The signals on the central reservation and the back of the hard shoulder apply to all lanes.

- The signals on gantries apply only to the lanes they are situated over.

- The signals are switched on to tell drivers what to do, or to alert them to hazards ahead. Always follow the instructions or the advice on the signals. They are there for the safety of you and other drivers.

- When the signals are not in operation they are blank. When they are in operation they flash either **amber** or **red** and use a matrix of white lights to display symbols or message such as FOG.

- The signals flash amber lights to warn drivers of hazards, temporary speed limits or lane diversions ahead.

Move into the lane on your left

Change lane now

You must stop

The two right-hand lanes are closed

- When the signals flash red it means you must stop. If the red flashing lights are on a signal in the central reservation or at the back of the hard shoulder, it applies to all lanes. If the red flashing lights are on a gantry, it means you must not go beyond the red light in that lane. In addition to the red flashing light there may also be a red X.

- See rules 170 to 173 of the Highway Code and the section on **Light signals controlling lights**.

STOPPING ON A MOTORWAY

You must not:

- **stop on the motorway**, except in an emergency or when instructed to by the police, an emergency sign or red flashing lights

- **stop to recover things** that have fallen from your vehicle

- **stop on the hard shoulder** to make or receive a telephone call, except in an emergency
- **park anywhere on a motorway**, including slip roads, hard shoulders and the central reservation
- **pick up or drop off passengers** anywhere on the motorway, including the slip road
- **walk on the carriageway**, except in an emergency.
- **cross the motorway**.

If anything falls from your vehicle that could be a danger to other drivers, do not try to remove it yourself. Stop at the next emergency telephone and tell the police. Do the same if you see something dangerous in the carriageway.

Stopping in an emergency

- Try to avoid stopping on the motorway because of mechanical problems. If you think you might have a problem, either pull into a service station or leave by the next exit.

- If you have to stop on the motorway because of an emergency, you need to know the advice given in the paragraphs on **Motorway breakdowns** in rules 183 and 184 of the Highway Code.

The motorway is a very hazardous place for anything not moving in the direction of the traffic flow. Standing still on the hard shoulder is dangerous for you and for other road users. The advice in the Highway Code is designed to get you and your vehicle

as far away from the traffic as possible. The key
points are:

• do not stop unless it is an emergency

• pull as far over to the left of the hard shoulder as
  possible

• put on your hazard warning lights

• get your passengers off the hard shoulder and on to
  the grass verge, well away from danger

• don't attempt any repairs yourself, not even changing
  a tyre

• telephone for help

• after you have telephoned for assistance wait near
  your vehicle, but well back on to the verge, along
  with any passengers

• if for any reason you have to stay in your vehicle,
  either on the carriageway or the hard shoulder, put
  on your hazard warning lights and keep your seat
  belt on.

Finding an emergency phone box on the motorway

• Emergency telephones, connected
  directly to the police, are placed
  along the motorways at about one
  mile intervals. The boxes are at the
  back of the hard shoulder and are
  coloured orange and white or orange
  and black and have a picture of a
  telephone on them.

• Small blue arrows on the 100 yard
  marker posts at the back of the hard
  shoulder point you in the direction of
  the nearest emergency telephone.

• You must never cross the motorway to
  use an emergency telephone on the other
  carriageway. You could either be injured or killed
  yourself or cause other people to be injured or killed.

EXIT SIGNS

Signs giving advance warning of exits follow a fairly
standard pattern on motorways.

At one mile	a direction sign giving junction number and the road number leading off the exit
At half a mile	a direction sign giving same information plus a destination name
At 300 yards	a 300 yards countdown marker, marking the distance to the start of the slip road
At 200 yards	a 200 yards countdown marker
At 100 yards	a 100 yards countdown marker
At the start of the slip road	A large direction board giving the junction number, road number, destination name plus the names of the main destinations ahead

Countdown markers at the exit from a motorway. Each bar represents 100 yards to the exit.

LEAVING THE MOTORWAY

• If you are not already in lane 1, start looking for an opportunity to move into it after you pass the one mile sign for the exit you want.

• Make sure you are in lane 1 well before your exit.

• Start indicating to leave the motorway at about the 300 yard marker post.

• Generally aim to lose speed in the deceleration lane of the slip road rather than on the motorway itself.

• As you drive down the slip road check your speed on the speedometer. Diving at high speeds for long periods distorts your perception of speed. You may think you are driving more slowly than you actually are. Keep on checking the speedometer until your sense of speed returns to normal.

• If you go past a motorway exit that you wanted, you have no option but to drive on to the next exit. You *must not* do a U-turn or reverse along any part of the motorway, including the hard shoulder.

7 Crossings, junctions and roundabouts

PEDESTRIAN CROSSINGS

The main types of pedestrian crossing are:
• zebra crossings
• pelican crossings
• puffin crossings.

As you approach a crossing:
• look for people waiting to cross
• if you see anyone, slow down and prepare to stop
• allow more time and space for stopping if the roads are slippery because of dust, rain, snow, ice or contaminants.

When you must stop
• At pelican and puffin crossings you must stop when instructed to by the lights.
• At zebra crossings you should anticipate when pedestrians are about to cross, and draw to a smooth stop to allow them to do so. You must stop if a pedestrian steps on to the crossing.

Zig-zag markings
• On each side of pedestrian crossings there are zig-zag markings.

- It is an offence to overtake on the crossing or within the zig-zags.
- It is an offence to park on the crossing or within the zig-zags.
- You may only stop on the crossing or within the zig-zags to allow pedestrians to cross, to prevent an accident or in circumstances beyond your control, such as when moving in queues of slow-moving, stop-go traffic.
- In slow-moving traffic you should try to judge the flow of the traffic so that you do not stop directly on the crossing. Always leave the crossing space clear for the pedestrians to cross.

Features of pedestrian crossings

The distinctive features of the three types of pedestrian crossing are listed below.

Zebra crossings
- Belisha beacons
- zig-zag stripes each side of the crossing
- black and white stripes across the road

Pelican crossings
- red and green figures
- zig-zag stripes each side of the crossing
- flashing green figures
- red lights

- amber lights
- green lights
- flashing amber lights
- road studs

- For the driver, pelican crossing lights are the same as ordinary traffic lights except that a flashing amber light follows the red light.
- The flashing amber light corresponds with a green flashing figure visible to pedestrians.
- While the amber light is flashing you must give way to pedestrians on the crossing. If there are no pedestrians you may go.

Puffin crossings
- red and green figures
- zig-zag stripes each side of the crossing
- red lights
- amber lights
- green lights
- red and amber lights together
- road studs

- For the driver, puffin crossing lights are the same as ordinary traffic lights. There are no flashing amber lights or flashing green figures.
- Puffin lights sense whether pedestrians are waiting and will only change to amber, and then red, if pedestrians wait to cross after the button has been pushed.

TRAFFIC CALMING

Speed humps and chicanes

Speed humps and other methods of traffic calming such as chicanes (narrowing and obstructing of the road to slow traffic) are becoming more familiar as communities and planners try to move the balance of road safety in favour of pedestrians.

• When you see any of these features (and think of rows of parked cars as unofficial traffic calming features), recognise that there are pedestrians around and adapt your driving accordingly.

Dealing with speed humps

• Generally there will be warning signs indicating traffic calming measures and saying what they are. This information is carried on a plate below the warning sign. See the Highway Code, **Traffic signs**.

• Warning signs will indicate when there are road humps.

- The humps themselves should be marked on the road with white painted triangles and edge lines. These are not required in 20 mph zones.

- You should already be travelling slowly when you approach a hump because you are in an area used by pedestrians.

- When you actually come to cross the humps, slow down even more. If you travel too fast you may lose control or cause damage to your steering or suspension.

LEVEL CROSSINGS

A level crossing is where a railway crosses the road. Some level crossings are controlled by lights, some have audible alarms, some have barriers and some have nothing other than a 'Give way' sign. Most have lights, barriers and an audible alarm. The triangular warning sign on the approach to a level crossing shows a gate if the crossing has barriers – or a puffing steam train if there are no barriers. When you see the warning sign, look for the crossing, slow down and be ready to stop.

Level crossing signals

- If no lights are showing at all on a level crossing controlled by lights, cross if your exit is clear.

- When the steady amber light shows and the alarm

sounds, stop if you have not already crossed the
white line, unless it is unsafe to do so.

- The steady amber light means stop before the white
  line unless it is unsafe to do so.

- Red flashing lights will join the amber light, and all
  three lights will continue to shine and the alarm
  continue to sound until the train has passed.

- If the red lights continue to flash after the train has
  passed and the alarm changes tone, continue to wait
  as another train is coming.

- Only move forward when all the lights go out, the
  alarm stops and the barriers are raised or gates
  opened.

- If you wait more than three minutes with the lights
  flashing and no train comes, or if you break down on
  the crossing, or if there is anything unusual or
  malfunctioning, phone the signalman.

The Highway Code advice on level crossings

- Never drive on to a level crossing until the exit is
  clear. Where there are yellow box markings on the
  road, do not enter the box unless your exit is clear.
- Never stop on a crossing.
- Never stop just beyond a crossing.
- Never drive over a crossing nose-to-tail.
- Never park near to a crossing.
- Never zig-zag between lowered barriers.

JUNCTIONS

Adapting your driving to the conditions is a key principle for safe driving. Some of the commonest features you will meet while driving are junctions. Junctions are hazardous because vehicles are moving across each other's paths and any interruption to the free flow of traffic is hazardous. Where this occurs, you need to identify the hazards, assess the risks and act to minimise them. 18% of drivers involved in accidents are turning when they have their accident. Right turns account for five times as many accidents as left turns. Note below the key to approaching junctions.

- *Observation* – look ahead for junctions, anticipate where they are going to be from gaps in the line of buildings, hedges and parked cars, from road signs, and from solitary street lamps which are often placed on the opposite side of the road from a junction. When you see a junction, look for other road users.

- *Position* – position for safety and for a good view.

- *Speed* – the less you can see the slower you should go. The narrower the roadspace, the slower you should go.

- In fog, you need to take extra care at junctions, see **9 Vehicle handling.**

- Where long vehicles are turning at junctions you need to allow them extra roadspace. See **10 Other vehicles.**

• Where junctions are obscured by parked vehicles and other obstructions you need to take extra care. See below.

Negotiating junctions

• As you approach a junction, look for other road users, assess their intentions and plan what to do.

• If the junction is blocked, slow down and be prepared to stop. Don't insist on ploughing through just because you have priority.

• In slow-moving traffic, you may find one or more vehicles blocking your path. Wait and let them go. Don't get angry and don't try to squeeze between them. Don't block junctions yourself or try to force other drivers to give way to you. Keep the junction clear and wait patiently for an opportunity to cross.

Parked vehicles may restrict your vision

Be aware of children concealed by parked vehicles

Busy junctions are often controlled by traffic lights and/or box junctions. See Box junctions below.

Traffic lights

- Traffic lights are relatively straightforward to deal with, so long as you understand and obey the sequence of lights. See **12 Signs and signals**.

- Always keep a watchful eye for other drivers who ignore or try to beat amber and red lights.

- Turning right at traffic lights can sometimes be a problem because of oncoming traffic. If you are waiting to turn right in the middle of the junction, you may do so during the amber phase, so long as you have already crossed the stop line.

Emerging at a junction

While waiting to emerge from a minor road at a junction, do not pull out so far that vehicles on the major road have to alter their course to get round you. Also take care not to position yourself so as to block the view of other drivers waiting to emerge, especially those to your left. Think about how your actions will affect other road users, especially pedestrians, cyclists and motorcyclists, who are at particular risk at junctions.

Emerging from an obscured junction

Junctions are often obscured by parked vehicles and overgrown foliage. You should take great care at obscured junctions. If you are on the side road:

• drive up to the junction slowly and stop with your front bumper at the point where the side road intersects with the main road

• look left and right along the major road

• if the road appears clear, edge forward looking both ways until you have a full view along the road

• give way to any road users on the major road

• when you can see that the way is clear, pull out firmly

• always give way to traffic on the road you are joining, and look carefully for cycles and motorcycles.

If you are on the major road:

- anticipate junctions by gaps in the rows of parked vehicles
- if you can do so safely, position your vehicle so that you are better able to see into the junction
- drive at a speed which would allow you to stop if a vehicle suddenly pulled out of the junction.

OTHER ROAD USERS AT JUNCTIONS

The Highway Code advises you to take extra care at junctions. This is because road users move across each other's paths and visibility is often reduced by buildings, vegetation, traffic and parked vehicles.
The Highway Code identifies road users who are at particular risk at junctions:

- pedestrians
- cyclists
- motorcyclists.

Pedestrians

- Pedestrians have to cross the road at junctions.
- They are at risk both from vehicles turning into the junction and from vehicles pulling out of it.
- Pedestrians often cross between vehicles queuing to pull out of a junction, so take care as you edge forward.
- **Before you turn into a junction, look for**

pedestrians crossing or about to cross.
• **If there are any pedestrians, give way to them.**
• **If your view into the junction is restricted by buildings or parked vehicles, slow right down.**
• **Before moving out of a junction, make sure that there are no pedestrians standing in front of your vehicle, or crossing your intended path.**

Cyclists and motorcyclists

Cyclists and motorcyclists are at particular risk from vehicles pulling out of junctions, and knocking them down or cutting across them.

You also have to allow greater safety margins when assessing their speed of approach. This really is important advice. Motorcyclists are 35 times more likely to be killed or seriously injured than drivers.

BOX JUNCTIONS

• Box junctions are indicated by yellow criss-cross lines painted on the road.
• They require you to think ahead as you approach them.
• You may enter a box junction only if your exit is clear, or if you want to turn right but your exit is blocked by oncoming traffic or other vehicles waiting to turn right.

If another driver incorrectly halts in a yellow-lined box junction, blocking your path, wait calmly until the junction is free. Do not lose your temper. Do not attempt to squeeze past.

CROSSROADS

- At unmarked crossroads – those without road markings or 'Give way' signs – no vehicle has priority, even where the roads are of different sizes.

- Take great care at unmarked crossroads and never assume you have right of way.

- If you can't see into the arms of the crossroads, slow right down.

- Vehicles turning right at crossroads are often involved in accidents, so look carefully and don't take risks.

Vehicles turning right across each other

- Where vehicles travelling in opposite directions both want to turn right at a crossroads, the safest course is normally to pass behind each other, offside to offside. See the Highway Code rules 118 and 119.

- Where this is not possible, great care needs to be taken when passing in front of each other, nearside to nearside.

- In this position, the other vehicle blocks the view of oncoming traffic.

- Whichever manoeuvre is used, it is essential that a clear view of the road to the left is obtained before crossing it.

ROUNDABOUTS

Roundabouts are easy to deal with so long as you get your observation, course, speed and signalling right. (See rules 123–128 of the Highway Code.) Give way to the right at the white dotted line across the entry to roundabouts, unless signs and road markings give you the right of way.

Approaching and negotiating a roundabout

- Decide which exit you are going to take. Indicate left to go left, right to go right or full circle. Do not indicate if you intend to go straight on.

- Follow any signs giving directions about which lane you should take. If there are no signs: approach in the left lane if you intend to go left; approach in the right lane if you intend to go right or to turn full circle. Approach in either lane if you intend to go straight on.

- Reduce your speed so that you are able to stop smoothly when you reach the roundabout.

- At the line across the entry to the roundabout, give way to any traffic already on the roundabout, stopping at the line if necessary.

- Move on to the roundabout.

Going left at a roundabout

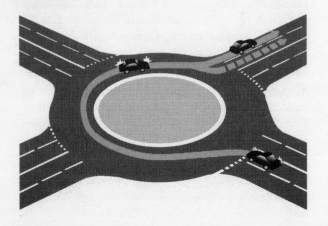

Going right at a roundabout

Signalling at a roundabout

• If you intend to turn left, take the left lane and keep
  your left indicator on until you have left the
  roundabout.

• If you intend to go right, keep your right indicator
  flashing and take the right lane until you pass the
  exit before the one you want. Check your mirrors
  and over your left shoulder, indicate left and move
  over to the left lane. Stay in the left lane and keep
  your left indicator flashing until you leave the
  roundabout.

• If you intend to go right round the roundabout,
  follow a similar course, moving over after the exit
  before the one you want.

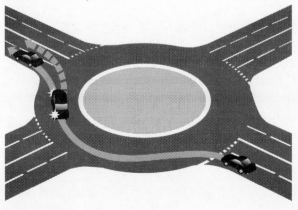

Going straight on at a roundabout

- If you intend to go straight on and you are in the left lane, take the left lane round the roundabout. Put on your left indicator after you have passed the exit before the one you want. Keep indicating until you have left the roundabout. Keep a check in your mirrors and over your right shoulder for vehicles moving across to leave by exits before yours.

- If you intend to go straight on and you are in the right lane, take the right lane until you have passed the exit before the one you want. Check your mirrors and over your left shoulder, indicate left and move over to the left lane. Stay in the left lane and keep the indicator flashing until you leave the roundabout.

Special cases

- Cyclists and horse riders may keep in the left lane all the way round a roundabout, whichever exit they intend to take.

- Long vehicles may take a course which straddles several lanes as they approach and negotiate a roundabout. Note their signals and give them plenty of room.

- On mini roundabouts, do not drive over the centre marking.

8 Vehicle safety

GENERAL SAFETY REQUIREMENTS

The law requires that your vehicle, load, passengers
and any trailer that you tow are safe. You must not
carry more passengers than is safe and you must carry
them in a safe manner. Safety is defined as not
involving any 'danger of injury to yourself or others'.

DRIVER AND PASSENGER SAFETY

Seat belts

• If there is a suitable seat belt available, passengers
and drivers must wear one unless they are exempt for
medical reasons.

• The driver is responsible for ensuring that any child
under 14 wears an appropriate restraint, if one is
available.

• Children under three may not go in the front
passenger seat without an appropriate child restraint.
The regulations governing children and restraints are
covered below.

Head restraints

• Head restraints are fixed into the back of car seats to
prevent your head whipping backwards when the car

is hit from behind. So-called 'whiplash' injuries can
be severe.

• It is important that the head restraint is at the right
  height for you.

• The top of the head restraint should be at
  approximately the level of your eyes. If the restraint
  is too low it might damage your neck in a collision.

• Get into the habit of checking the head restraint
  height when you put on your seat belt.

Clothing

Clothing has its part to play in driving safety.

• Generally you should wear clothes that allow you
  free movement and unrestricted access to the
  controls.

• If you are going on a long journey, wear comfortable
  clothing to reduce physical fatigue.

• The most important items of clothing are your shoes.
  Wear shoes that make it easy to feel and control the
  pedals. Otherwise you may get your pedals in a
  tangle during an emergency.

Child restraints

Each year, 500 children are needlessly killed or
seriously injured in car accidents because they are not
properly restrained. As the driver, you are legally
responsible for ensuring that all children under 14

travelling in the car are properly restrained in accordance with the law. Remember, whatever the parents or other relatives say, you are responsible in law. Your responsibilities are as follows.

Children under three

• Young children must have an appropriate child restraint (see below) if travelling in the front.

• If the only appropriate child restraint is in the front, the child must be placed in the front restraint.

• If there are no proper child restraints, generally the child is safest wearing an adult seat belt in the back.

Children from three to eleven and less than 1.5 m (5 ft) tall

• Children must wear an appropriate child restraint if one is available, whether they travel in the front or the back.

• If the only appropriate child restraint is in the front, the child must be placed in the front restraint.

• If no appropriate child restraint is available, children must wear adult seat belts

12 and 13 year old children, and younger children taller than 1.5 m (5 ft)

• Older children must wear adult seat belts if they are available.

Appropriate child restraints

The Highway Code defines an appropriate child
restraint as:

• 'a baby carrier, child seat, harness or booster seat
appropriate to the child's weight'. This is the
definition that you will be tested on in the theory
test, so you need to know it for the test.

The Department of Transport publication, *Choosing
Safety*, defines a child restraint as a properly designed
and tested baby or child seat.

• It explains that there are many different types of
restraint available, including baby seats, child seats,
booster seats and booster cushions.

• An appropriate restraint is one that is suitable for the
weight, size and height of your child.

• It advises that rear-facing baby seats are safest for
babies up to 10 kg (22 lb). It says these are also
called rear-facing infant carriers. These should not be
confused with carrycots.

• Carrycot restraints do not provide adequate
protection and are generally not recommended. Use
them only when no other form of restraint is
available.

Dangerous travelling positions for children

• Never allow a child to travel in the boot or in the
luggage area of a hatchback.

- Never use a rear-facing baby seat in the the front seat of a car that has an airbag fitted on the passenger side. The expanding airbag could cause a serious or fatal injury to the baby.

- Never place a baby or child between yourself and your seat belt. If you crashed at 30 mph your body would crush your baby with a force of $3\frac{1}{2}$ tons, enough to kill or seriously injure it.

- Never allow a child to stand, looking between the two front seats. In a frontal collision the child will hit the windscreen at more or less the speed of the car at the time of the accident.

Adults (anyone over 14)

- Adult passengers are responsible for complying with the law themselves.

- They must wear a seat belt if one is available, whether they are travelling in the front or the rear.

- As the driver you must wear a seat belt if one is available, unless you are exempt on medical grounds.

Child locks

- Most cars are now fitted with child lock levers on the rear doors.

- When the lock is set, it prevents the door being opened from inside the vehicle.

- Children are inquisitive and do not realise how

dangerous it is to open a door while the car is
moving. So if you have young children travelling in
the car, set the child locks.

VEHICLE LOADING

As the driver, you are legally responsible for ensuring
the safety of any loads you carry or tow. The Highway
Code gives the following advice. Any loads carried or
towed:
• must be secure
• must not stick out dangerously
• must not overload your vehicle or trailer.

Roof racks

• Roof racks must be securely fastened to the car and
  loads must be securely fastened to the roof rack
  during transit.

• As far as possible try to keep any loads, whether
  carried in the vehicle or on the roof rack, evenly
  balanced. Additional loads will affect the balance and
  handling of the car.

• Take any additional loads into account while
  cornering, and especially while braking – it takes
  longer to stop when the vehicle has additional loads.

Caravans and trailers

• Loads in caravans and trailers should be well secured

and evenly distributed. Loads which move about in
transit can be very destabilising.

• You must not allow anyone to travel in a caravan
  while it is being towed.

• The laden weight of a caravan or trailer should
  preferably not exceed 85% of the kerbside weight of
  the towing vehicle, and should definitely not exceed
  the actual kerbside weight.

• The national speed limits for cars towing caravans or
  trailers are lower than for cars alone: 50 mph on
  unrestricted single carriageways and 60 mph on
  unrestricted dual carriageways and motorways.

• You may not use the outside lane of motorways to
  tow caravans or trailers unless the other lanes are
  closed.

• You must not leave a caravan or trailer parked on the
  road at night without lights.

Swerving, snaking and winds

If a caravan or trailer begins to swerve or snake while
driving along:
• gently ease off the accelerator and gradually slow
  down
• do not try to brake sharply or steer sharply to
  counteract the swinging
• be wary of strong winds and crosswinds. On windy
  days reduce your speed, and if you can, avoid
  exposed places.

ROADWORTHINESS

The law requires you to keep your vehicle roadworthy.
Items which the Highway Code identifies as having to
be in good condition and in working order for your
vehicle to be roadworthy include:
• lights
• brakes
• steering
• tyres, including spare
• exhaust system
• seat belts and fittings
• windscreens and windows
• demisters, windscreen wipers and washers
• speedometer
• horn.

The following must be kept clean and clear:
• windscreens and windows
• lights, indicators and reflectors; headlights must be
  properly adjusted to prevent dazzle
• mirrors
• number plates.

Before you set off, your seat, seat belt, head restraint
and mirrors must be correctly adjusted.

Regular maintenance

Your car should be roadworthy whenever you drive it .
Maintain it at regular intervals

- Inspect it regularly and make sure that the brake fluid, clutch fluid and water coolant reservoirs are fully topped up.

- If your car is more than three years old (four years old in Northern Ireland), it must have an MOT.

- Never take an MOT as a guarantee of roadworthiness, MOTs last for a year; cars need maintaining all the time.

POWER CHECK

Get into the habit of doing a POWER check each day. POWER spells the first letters of the items you should check to make sure they are in working order:

Petrol   Adequate fuel, petrol or diesel, for your journey.

Oil   Engine oil is properly topped up and the oil warning light goes out immediately the engine starts.

Water   Radiator reservoir correctly filled, windscreen wash reservoirs full. Appropriate antifreeze in both during cold weather.

Electrics Battery is sound; lights, brakelights, indicators, horn, gauges, warning lights, windscreen wipers, demister, screen washer all working properly.

Rubber   Wiper blade is working properly and tyres are correctly inflated, with legal tread depth, undamaged walls and treads.

Start-up check

Before every journey, do a **Start-up check**. When you
turn on the ignition, a series of warning lights should
light up and then go out as the engine starts and you
move away. If the warning lights do not light up in the
first place, or fail to go out once the vehicle is moving,
they need checking. Warning lights you might expect
to find are:

• ignition warning light, usually red
• oil pressure warning light, usually orange
• brake fluid level warning light
• brake pad wear warning light
• parking brake (handbrake) warning light
• ABS warning light.

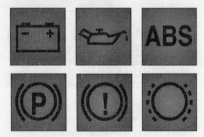

Gauges and warning lights

You should know the meaning of the gauges and
warning lights on your dashboard, and use them.

• If a warning light comes on, pull in somewhere safe
  and find out what the problem is.

- Don't ignore a warning light. If you ignore the oil pressure warning light your engine could seize up. If the ignition warning light remains lit, the battery is not being re-charged and you will run out of electric power. If the water temperature gauge is in the warning area, the engine may boil over or seize up.

Odd smells and uneasy feelings

- If you smell something, stop somewhere safe and find out what it is. Fire can spread with alarming speed, so don't take risks. Always check.
- Similarly if something feels or sounds odd, check it out. Listen to that uneasy voice in the back of your mind. It could save you a lot of money and might even save your life.
- Avoid the temptation to say to yourself 'Oh it just does that'. Always check. There's always a reason.

TYRES AND SUSPENSION

Radials and cross-plys

There are two types of tyres: radials and cross-plys. Make sure you know which type you have on your car.

- Radials and cross-plys are constructed differently and behave differently. If they are used in the wrong combination they could cause your car to go out of control.
- It is illegal to mix radials and cross-plys on the same axle, and unsafe to put radials on the front wheels

and cross-plys on the rear
wheels.

• It is safest to use tyres of one
type only on your car.

• Radials give a better grip in
the wet, and generally modern
cars are fitted with radials.

• There are still many cross-plys around, so you should
check carefully when you fit replacements to make
sure that they are compatible with the existing tyres.

Tyre condition and tread

• Tyres must be free from cuts and other defects.

• Car tyres must have a tread depth of at least 1.6 mm
continuously round the tyre and across three-quarters
of the tyre width.

• Make sure the valves have dust caps fitted.

Tyre inflation

• You must inflate your tyres properly.

• If you do not, your braking and steering will be
seriously affected.

• Inflate the tyres to the pressures recommended in the
car's handbook, making adjustments for weight and
speed as given.

• Pressures should be read before you set off when the
tyres are cold, not mid-way through your journey
when they have warmed up.

- Warm tyres can give distorted readings.
- Check and adjust the pressures of your tyres regularly – at least once a week – and don't forget to include your spare tyre in the checks.

Looking after your tyres

- Inspect your tyres regularly and keep them properly inflated.
- Avoid driving over potholes and do not drive over the kerb or scuff the tyre wall along the edge of kerbstones – it could rupture the wall of the tyre.
- If there are any cuts, bulges or splits on the tyre, swap it for the spare and have it inspected.

Uneven tread wear

- Scuffing, uneven or rapid wear of the tyre treads indicates that there is a problem with your car. It could be the brakes, the alignment, the suspension or the steering.
- Your car might be in a dangerous condition.
- Have your car investigated and repaired by a competent person as soon as possible.

Flat and burst tyres

- If you have a flat tyre, gently bring your car to a stop as soon as you safely can at the side of the road.
- If it is safe, replace the tyre with the spare.

- Don't attempt to change a tyre on the hard shoulder of a motorway.

- If your tyre bursts while you are driving, The Highway Code additional information advises you to 'grip the steering wheel firmly and allow the vehicle to roll to a stop at the side of the road'.

Suspension

- If your car rolls a lot on corners or if the bonnet seems to bounce a lot when you go over uneven ground, it might mean that the shock absorbers are failing.

- Check by bouncing the car up and down by each corner in turn.

- If the car bounces for more than two bounces after you let go, have the shock absorber on that corner checked and repaired.

- Weak shock absorbers are dangerous. They affect your control of the car during braking and steering. Get them replaced.

BRAKES

- Your car is only legal if your brakes and your brakelights are fully working.

- If either your brakes or brakelights are not working, you must not use the car until you have got them repaired.

- Get into the habit of regularly checking your brakelights – you'll need someone to help you.

- Every time you set off in the car, keep your speed down until you are certain your car is braking properly.

The importance of brakelights

It's obvious why defective brakes are dangerous but it might not be immediately apparent why defective brakelights are dangerous.

- Lit brakelights are probably the commonest signal that we give on the road.

- They tell other road users that we are slowing down or stopping, allowing them to take appropriate action.

- It is easy not to think of brakelights as signals because we don't have to do anything to put them on. Try to think instead of the brake pedal as having a dual function – it gives a slowing down signal and it puts the brakes on.

- Without brakelight signals, other drivers would find it much harder to recognise when we are slowing down.

- This is why a safe following distance behind the vehicle in front is of such importance. You can be sure that your own brakelights are working properly but you can never be sure that the brakelights on the vehicle in front are working until you see them.

Brake maintenance

Brakes work on a hydraulic system. When you put your foot on the brake pedal, you pump brake fluid through pipes into small piston cylinders at each brake. The pistons expand, forcing friction pads (brake pads or shoes) against the wheels. This stops the wheels turning, thereby stopping the car. If there is insufficient brake fluid, or if the fluid leaks, the system will not work. Equally, if the friction linings are worn out, the brakes will not work.

- Check your brake fluid reservoir at least weekly to make sure it is fully topped up.

- If the fluid level starts to drop, or you find brake fluid leaks or your brakes start to feel soft, get your brakes checked immediately.

- Regularly check your brake pads or brake shoes. They are designed to wear out and be replaced.

The parking brake (handbrake) does not usually use hydraulics, but uses brake cables instead. Check that your handbrake can hold the car stationary on hills. If it can't, or if it only holds right at the end of its travel, have it adjusted by a competent person.

Uneven braking and pulling to the side

- If your car brakes unevenly – pulls to one side, instead of braking in a straight line – it probably means that your brakes need attention. Have your brakes checked and repaired as soon as possible.

- If your car pulls to one side as you drive*, the brakes probably need adjusting. However, this pull could also be caused by tyre, steering, suspension or alignment problems, so have the car inspected by a competent mechanic as soon as possible. Don't drive the car until it is repaired.

*Try not to confuse this with the effect of the road camber. Where the camber slopes down to the left, as it usually does, all cars will tend to be gradually drawn to the left. This 'drift' is corrected by a firm hold on the steering wheel. Where the road is flat this slight drift to the left should not occur. If it does, and it is not explained by the wind, get your vehicle checked

FUEL, POLLUTION AND NOISE

Fuel

- Petrol and diesel are inflammable and toxic substances. Care needs to be taken in their use and storage.

- Avoid getting either on your clothing or skin and avoid breathing in their vapours.

- Petrol vapours, especially unleaded petrol vapours, may contain cancer-causing agents, so it is important that the passenger compartment does not smell of petrol vapours.

- Generally your car should not smell of fuel. If it does, have it checked.
- If you suddenly smell fuel while driving, stop as soon as you can safely do so, and investigate.
- Check for leaks in the fuel pipes and where the pipe goes into the fuel tank, fuel pump and engine. Do not continue until you are certain it is safe.
- Get it checked by a competent mechanic as soon as possible.
- The threat of fire in a car is very real. You must do all you can to avoid it.

Fuel and smoking

Never smoke where there is a possibility of igniting fuel or fuel vapours because of the danger of fire and explosion. Never smoke when:
- inspecting the car
- looking for fuel leaks
- working on the car
- refuelling the car
- in a petrol station.

Fuel containers

- Fuel must only be carried in specifically designated fuel cans.
- It is illegal to put fuel in any other type of container. The illustrations on the next page show a designated container for petrol and for diesel.

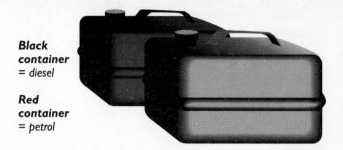

Black container = *diesel*

Red container = *petrol*

Use the right type of fuel

Before going on a journey, check your fuel gauge after it has settled down, and make sure you have enough fuel for your journey. Avoid running out of fuel. It can be dangerous if you are in a stream of traffic, and may suck sludge into the fuel line from the bottom of the tank.

- Make sure you re-fuel with the right fuel.

- Putting petrol in a diesel engine or diesel in a petrol engine can damage the engine.

- Using leaded petrol in an engine with a catalytic convertor will ruin the convertor: use only unleaded fuel.

- You can't always tell by looking at a car what fuel it will use. Always check with the manual or the owner, and also check that the fuel line you are using is the correct type. Fuel pumps, lines and pump handles are generally colour-coded:

    red   leaded petrol

green   unleaded petrol
black   diesel

Be careful: some pumps have several lines, each
supplying different fuels.

Pollution and noise

Exhaust emissions

• Exhaust emissions are regulated by law to prevent
  pollution.
• Correct tuning of your engine minimises the
  production of pollutants.
• Vehicles registered after 1975 have to pass an
  exhaust emissions test at their MOT to make sure
  they are below government limits.
• It is illegal to drive a vehicle (to which the
  legislation applies) which exceeds the limits.

Noise

• Noise is another form of pollution.

• You are required by law to have an effective silencer
  which reduces noise to reasonable levels.

• Avoid causing excessive noise at night by over-
  revving your engine, slamming car doors or sounding
  your horn.

• You must not sound your horn in built-up areas
  between 11.30 pm and 7 am.

9 Vehicle handling

To drive safely, it is essential to adapt your driving to the actual conditions. Road conditions, weather conditions and daylight conditions determine how fast you can go, what position you should be in, what following distances are safe and whether you should be out on the roads at all. They affect visibility, steering and braking and the time that your journey will take – you must take them all into account. This chapter looks at handling your car in different situations and circumstances.

MOVING OFF SAFELY FROM A PARKED POSITION

Moving off safely depends on good observation and making your intentions clear to other road users. To move off safely:
- use your mirrors to check what is going on behind you
- wait for a safe gap in the traffic
- signal if necessary
- look round for a final check before you move off
- only move off when it is safe.

The Highway Code says the purpose of signalling is to help and warn other road users, including pedestrians.

- When moving off, wait until a safe gap appears in the traffic and then signal.

- Do not signal in the hope that other drivers will slow down, or while you are waiting for a safe gap to occur in the traffic.

SAFE BRAKING

It is important to be able to slow down and stop safely with your car fully under control. Safe braking is the key to this.

- Controlled braking requires good observation and anticipation so that you start braking in good time. If you are not paying attention to the road and to other road users, you won't be able to do this.

- In normal conditions the safest way to brake is to start lightly, steadily increase the pressure as speed is lost, and then ease off just before stopping. This is called progressive braking.

- Declutch just before stopping or the engine will stall.

- Keeping the clutch engaged during braking helps to slow the car through engine braking, which is why the gears should remain engaged.

- When the car has fully stopped, the handbrake can be applied if appropriate.

- Applying the handbrake before the car has stopped might lock the rear wheels and cause a skid.

Tyre grip and safe braking

Your ability to brake safely depends on your tyre grip. If you exceed the tyre grip available, you will skid and lose control over the direction of your vehicle. Tyre grip is dealt with later in this chapter but note the key points in relation to braking.

• When the weather or contaminants increase the slipperiness of the road surface, adjust your stopping distances to allow for the extra distance required because of reduced tyre grip.

• Avoid braking while steering. Generally you should reduce your speed to the correct speed for a corner or bend before you start to steer.

MANOEUVRING YOUR VEHICLE

Reversing your vehicle

Follow these guidelines for reversing.

• Make sure there are no obstructions behind you. Check carefully for pedestrians, especially children, who may be difficult to see because of their height.

• Know what is in your blind spot. Look round and use your mirrors, move your head to minimise the areas into which you cannot see.

• If you cannot see clearly, get out and look, or ask someone to help you.

• Reverse carefully, looking mainly through the rear

window but check all round, using the mirrors as
necessary. Remember that the front end swings out
as you reverse round a corner. Check that there is
nothing in its way.

- You must not reverse further than is necessary.

- Never reverse from a side road on to a main road.

- Avoid reversing out of a driveway on to the road. It
  is better to reverse in and drive out of driveways.

Turning in the road

- Turning in the road uses both sides of the road, takes
  time and may involve reversing, so it could present a
  hazard for other road users.

- Before you turn, check all round to make sure you
  will not get in the way of other road users.

- Turning round in a busy road can be dangerous. It is
  generally better to find a side road or other opening.

- Before you reverse into a side road check for the
  presence of pedestrians, especially children.
  Reversing into a driveway can also be hazardous if
  the view is restricted by walls or hedges.

- The Highway Code says that pavements are for
  people, not for vehicles. So neither the front nor the
  back of your car should overhang the pavement
  while you are turning – it could be a danger to
  pedestrians.

Negotiating obstructions on your side of the road

• Where there are obstructions on your side of the road, give way to oncoming vehicles.

• Stop far enough back from the obstruction to get a clear view past it and to give you an easy course when you move forward.

• Don't wave on or use any other unofficial signal to oncoming vehicles. Position yourself correctly and wait patiently.

• Don't forget to check in your mirrors before pulling out to go round the obstacle.

OVERTAKING

Overtaking is potentially dangerous because it could bring you into conflict with oncoming vehicles, vehicles overtaking you, vehicles pulling out and vehicles turning right. Overtaking needs to be considered and carried out carefully for it to be safe. Learn rules 99–106 of the Highway Code thoroughly and apply them. Always make full use of **MSM PSL**, before you overtake.

See **4 Recognising hazards** to refresh your memory of the **MSM PSL** procedure.

If you are in any doubt, do not overtake.

You must not overtake
- if you would cross or straddle a double white line which is unbroken on your side of the road
- in the zig-zag area of a pedestrian crossing
- between a 'No overtaking' sign and the sign cancelling it.

Do not overtake in the following circumstances because your vision will be restricted
- corners and bends
- hump-back bridges
- approaching the brow of a hill.

Do not overtake where you might come into conflict with other road users
- where there are road junctions on either side of the road.
- where the road narrows
- approaching a school crossing patrol
- where you would have to drive over diagonal white stripes or chevrons
- where you would have to enter a lane restricted for other vehicles, for example bus lanes
- on the inside of a bus or tram waiting at a stop
- where there are traffic queues at junctions or road works

- where you would cause another road user to change speed or direction
- at a level crossing.

Overtaking on the left

Generally, do not overtake on the left. However, there are three situations where you may overtake on the left:

- when the vehicle in front is signalling to turn right and it is safe to overtake on the left
- when traffic is moving in queues and the queue to your right is moving more slowly than you. Do not change lanes to enable you to overtake
- one-way streets.

Overtaking on dual carriageways

Before moving to overtake on dual carriageways and motorways:

- look in your mirrors and make sure there are no vehicles coming up behind you
- if a vehicle behind is moving up to overtake you, wait till it has passed before moving out to overtake yourself
- do not start indicating to overtake until it has passed
- if a signal would help other road users, indicate before you start to change position.

Being overtaken

• If someone is trying to overtake you should try and assist them.

• Keep to a steady speed, within the speed limit.

• If it is safe to do so, pull over and let the vehicle pass.

• Never try to prevent a vehicle overtaking by moving out or by increasing your speed.

• Hindering an overtaking vehicle is very dangerous.

• Don't regard yourself as a self-appointed policeman and try to block someone travelling faster than the speed limit.

Being followed too closely

• If you are in a line of traffic and the vehicle behind is too close for comfort, gradually increase your distance from the vehicle in front.

• This will make it easier for the vehicle behind to overtake, and allow you to brake more gently if you need to.

• Don't allow the vehicle behind to force you into exceeding the speed limit or driving faster than you think is safe.

• If it is legal and safe to do so, pull over and let the vehicle pass.

If someone overtakes you and pulls in too closely in front

- Assess whether you have a sufficiently safe following distance.

- If there is not a safe following distance between you and the new vehicle in front, drop back until there is.

- Remember the gap needs to be much greater in wet conditions.

HILLS

Road conditions

The type of road and whether it is hilly or flat are major considerations that you must take into account in your driving. The main safety considerations to bear in mind on hills are:

- it takes longer to stop going downhill

- you should never overtake just before the crest of a hill

- when you park on a hill, you should put on the handbrake, select a low gear and turn the wheels into the kerb.

The way to drive downhill is:

- brake to the correct speed for the hill before you begin to descend

- engage a low gear to control your speed before you begin to descend

- never coast downhill, either with the gears in neutral or your engine declutched. When you coast you lose control over the speed of your vehicle and you might find it difficult to re-engage the gear

- brake on the straight stretches

- avoid braking all the way down, because it wears out the brakes and can cause them to 'fade'(lose their braking ability). Use low gears to control your speed.

Note the proper sequence: ***brake first and then select a lower gear***. If you select a lower gear without first reducing your speed, you will cause the car to jolt when you re-engage the clutch.

Mechanical considerations

Use of the clutch

- Generally, whether you are on hills or not, do not drive along with the clutch depressed, because it reduces your control of the car.

- When you declutch to change gear, only hold the clutch down long enough to change gear smoothly.

- While the clutch is depressed you lose the power to accelerate, you lose engine braking and your steering becomes less responsive. If a sudden danger arose, each of these might be crucial.

Use of the gears

- Low gears turn the wheels with great power but at low speeds.
- High gears turn the wheels at high speed but with low power.
- First is the lowest gear and fourth the highest. In cars with five forward gears, fifth is the highest.
- The reverse gear is also a low gear.
- First gear is used for starting off, moving slowly in dense traffic and climbing very steep hills. High gears are used for cruising at speed and to help prevent wheel spin in snow.

TYRE GRIP

Whatever road you are on, you need to be able to keep your car under control and be able to stop in the distance you can see to be clear. Your ability to steer and your stopping distance depend on your tyre grip.

The grip of your tyres depends on:
- how the tyres were made
- the depth of tread over the entire contact area
- proper inflation.

Keep a safe distance from the vehicle in front

The grip of the road surface depends on:
• the material the road is made from, and whether it is worn smooth or not
• whether the road is slippery from rain, snow or ice
• whether the road is slippery because of road surface contaminants such as oil, diesel, mud and dust.

Where the road surface is slippery, you should drive slowly, accelerate and brake gently and steer smoothly. Avoid braking and steering, or accelerating and steering, at the same time.

WEATHER CONDITIONS

Weather conditions affect your driving in four ways:
• Cold and wet conditions might make it difficult to start the car.
• In rain, keep away from the spray of other vehicles. It reduces your visibility.

Drive at a speed which allows you to stop in the distance you can see to be clear

- Fog, snow and rain reduce visibility.
- Rain, snow and ice reduce tyre grip and therefore reduce your ability to accelerate, brake or steer, making skidding more likely.

THE WEATHER AND VISIBILITY

- Rain and snow reduce visibility while they are falling. The heavier they are, the more they reduce visibility.
- Spray, especially spray from lorries on fast roads, seriously reduces visibility.

Rain and snow

When rain, snow or wet roads reduce visibility:
- Make sure you can be seen: put on your dipped headlights.

- You must put on your headlights or front foglights if visibility falls below 100 metres.

- If visibility falls below 100 metres put on your rear foglights.

- You must switch off your foglights as soon as visibility improves because they may mask your brakelights and dazzle other drivers.

- Use your windscreen wipers, screen washers and demisters to keep your windows clear.

- Drive at a speed which allows you to stop in the distance you can see to be clear.

- Keep a safe distance from the vehicle in front.

- If the vehicle behind is following too closely, increase your distance from the vehicle in front.

- If you can avoid spray by following at a greater distance or driving in a different lane, do so.

- Do not drive with iced-up or misted windows. De-ice or demist them before you set out.

Spray from lorries

In wet weather, the tyres of lorries throw up large amounts of spray, especially when travelling fast. This makes it difficult for car and other drivers to see what is happening. The spray is worst close to the lorry. So in wet weather keep well back from the swirl of spray thrown up by the vehicle in front.

Keep well back from vehicles throwing up spray

• It allows you to see better.

• It provides you with a longer stopping distance, which you need in wet weather.

• It allows the lorry driver to see your dipped headlights through the cab mirrors.

Use dipped headlights

• Heavy spray also reduces what other drivers can see.

• Switch on your dipped headlights to make your car more visible to other drivers.

Overtaking in spray

• As you move forward to overtake a lorry in wet conditions, anticipate that the spray from the lorry will obscure your view.

• Switch your wipers to their fastest speed.

• In heavy spray, expect your view to be momentarily washed out as you draw past the back wheels of the lorry.

Fog

Fog can be very dangerous. You should read and make yourself thoroughly familiar with the Highway Code **Fog code**, rule 58, and **Fog lights**, rules 131 and 133. Make sure you keep sufficient distance between yourself and the vehicle in front, and to travel at a

speed which would allow you to stop in the distance
you can see to be clear.

Before you set out in fog:
• Make sure that your windscreen, windows and lights
  are clean.
• Make sure your lights, including brakelights,
  windscreen wipers, windscreen washers and
  demisters are in good working order.

When visibility is below 100 metres:
• You must use headlights or front foglights
• You are advised to use front and rear foglights.
  Switch them off when visibility improves. You *must
  not* use foglights at other times.

Improve your view through the windscreen by using
your:
• windscreen wipers
• windscreen washers (in freezing weather make sure
  you use the appropriate antifreeze in the wash
  solution)
• demisters.

When you slow down or brake in fog:
• use your brakes so that your brake lights warn the
  vehicles behind that you are slowing down
• brake gently to give following vehicles time to react.
  You will only be able to do this if you have sufficient
  distance between yourself and the vehicle in front.

Follow the advice on roadsigns:

• If roadsigns warn of fog, yet conditions appear to be clear, don't assume that they will remain clear. Fog is often patchy. Drifting banks of fog can suddenly immerse you in thick fog when it might look as though the fog is clearing.

Dipped headlights in fog

• Although the Fog code says you must use headlights or front foglights if visibility is below 100 metres, this does not imply that you are not to use headlights if visibility is above 100 metres.

• When mist, fog, rain or snow reduces visibility, use dipped headlights to make it easier for other road users to see you.

• Dipped headlights are best because full beam lights reflect off the fog, rain or snow, making it harder to see.

• Only use foglights when visibility is below 100 metres.

Junctions in fog

• Approach junctions with special care in fog.

• Before crossing, stop in the correct position, look carefully for other vehicles, wind down your window and listen for them.

• When you decide it is safe to go, move decisively.

• Don't stop where you would be in the path of approaching vehicles.

Parking in fog

• In fog there is always a danger if you park on the
  road that another road user will drive into you, so
  where possible park off the road in fog.

• Where this is not possible, park in the direction of
  the traffic flow, make sure your lights are clean and
  leave your sidelights on.

THE WEATHER AND TYRE GRIP

The effectiveness of your steering and braking
depends on your tyre grip. When tyre grip is reduced
skidding becomes more likely. Stopping distances are
increased by up to four times in wet conditions and by
up to ten times in snow, icy and near-freezing
conditions.

Conditions which make the roads slippery and reduce
tyre grip include:

• wetness, because of rain, slush or flooding

• snow

• ice or near-freezing conditions

• hot weather, because of dust or because the tar melts
  in the heat

• contamination, by oil, diesel, mud, etc.

All these conditions reduce your ability to steer, brake
and accelerate.

- If you steer too sharply or brake too harshly in slippery conditions your car may go into a skid.

- Acceleration also depends on tyre grip. If you accelerate too harshly in slippery conditions, your wheels may spin.

- Whenever the road surface is slippery you should accelerate, brake and steer very smoothly.

- On bends and corners slow down before you reach the bend, avoid any jerkiness in the use of the controls and use the highest gear you can.

Wet roads

- When the roads are wet during rain, after rain or because of some other cause, they will be more slippery than normal.

- Stopping distances can be up to four times longer on a wet road than on a dry road.

- Drive more slowly, steer more gently, allow a greater distance between you and the vehicle in front and brake more gently.

- If someone follows too closely or cuts in too closely in front of you, increase the gap between yourself and the vehicle in front.

- Be particularly wary of rain after a long hot dry spell. The rain mixes with the road dust to form an extremely slippery slurry.

Aquaplaning

• If your steering becomes light, it means a wedge of
  water is building up between your tyres and the road
  surface. This is called aquaplaning.

• To regain grip, slow down gradually by gently easing
  off the accelerator.

• Do not brake and do not alter your steering until you
  have regained grip. Then do everything with the
  lightest of touches.

What you must try to avoid is braking or steering so
sharply that you go into a skid. Skids are difficult to
control, especially in the limited space available on
most roads. When the roads are wet, anticipate the
risks of skidding and drive more gently.

Snow and ice

• Snow and ice make the roads considerably more
  slippery than rain. It can take up to ten times longer
  than normal to stop in snow and ice. So always
  consider whether your journey is really necessary.

If you do drive in snow, ice and near-freezing
conditions, follow this advice.

• Keep your speed down, and allow extra distance
  between yourself and the vehicle in front.

• Drive slowly, with low revs and in as high a gear as
  possible. This helps to avoid wheelspin.

• Steer, brake and accelerate as gently as possible.

Sudden changes in speed or direction could cause you to skid.

- Avoid braking on bends and corners.
- Brake gently on the straights.
- Reduce your speed before you enter bends or corners and drive round them slowly.
- Steer gently and smoothly round bends and corners.
- Leave a good distance between you and the vehicle in front.

Black ice

- Listen to local weather forecasts in cold weather.
- Take particular care if black ice is forecast. You will know when you are on black ice because your steering will become light.
- If tyre grip is suddenly reduced by black ice, you will feel the steering become lighter and the tyre noise go quieter.
- Gently ease back the accelerator, do not make any sudden steering movements, do not brake. If you are braking in a non-ABS car (see below), ease off the brakes.

Skidding

The best advice on skidding is not to get into a skid in the first place. In slippery conditions:

- drive slowly

- drive smoothly
- don't brake on corners
- don't steer or brake harshly
- don't steer and brake at the same time.

ABS – Antilock braking system

Some cars have an antilock braking system fitted. This system prevents the wheels locking when you brake heavily. The main benefit of these systems is that they help to maintain the ability to steer under heavy braking. They may also improve the effectiveness of the braking.

- When the ABS system comes into operation, you will feel a juddering.

- It is important to expect this as it is the way the system works.

- Do not take your foot off the brakes when you feel it. Keep your foot firmly down until you have braked sufficiently.

If your driving does cause the ABS to come into operation, take it as a warning. It means you are driving too fast for the conditions and that your observations are not as good as they should be. Reduce your speed and observe more carefully.

Cadence braking

Cadence braking is a special way of braking on slippery surfaces in cars not fitted with ABS. It is used

when you are starting to skid and you need to both
lose speed and steer at the same time.

• To use this technique, rhythmically and repetitively
  apply and release your brakes, while steering in the
  direction you wish to travel.

• The car slows when the brakes are applied and steers
  while they are released.

• Cadence braking is similar to the effect of ABS.

• If your car is fitted with ABS do not use cadence
  braking.

What to do if you do find yourself going into a skid

First, remove the cause of the skid.

• If you were braking release the brakes, except in cars
  fitted with ABS brakes.

• If you were accelerating, release the accelerator.

• Never brake in a skid unless your car is fitted with
  ABS or you are using cadence braking.

Next, regain directional control.

• Steer in the direction of the skid until you regain
  control, then gently steer back on course. The same
  advice applies to **rear wheel skids** – steer into the
  skid until you regain control and then gently steer
  back on to course.

Finally, continue more carefully.

- Once on course, very, very gradually begin to accelerate.
- Steer, brake and accelerate very smoothly.

Skids are difficult to control. The best advice is to avoid skids by adapting your driving to the conditions.

FORDS AND FLOODS

- Fords or floods may soak your brakes, making them ineffective.

- After a ford, test your brakes to make sure they are working before you continue driving at normal speeds.
- If they are not working properly, dry them out by gently braking while you drive slowly.
- Once they are dry you can return to an appropriate speed for the conditions.

WINDS

Crosswinds can be dangerous on exposed stretches of road, especially exposed stretches coming immediately after shelter. On windy days anticipate the problems created by crosswinds and anticipate the additional problems it causes for other road users.

- It is not unknown for strong winds to pick up small children and blow them into the road.
- Cyclists are very vulnerable to strong winds and are easily blown off course.
- Motorcyclists may be easily blown off course, especially when travelling at speed and overtaking big lorries.
- Vehicles with trailers are likely to be blown about.
- High-sided vehicles may be blown off course or be blown over.

In all these cases keep well behind vulnerable road users, and when you pass them keep well to the side. Give them space.

NIGHT AND LOW LIGHT CONDITIONS

- At night and in low light you should be able to stop in the distance you can see to be clear.
- If the only light is the light from your headlights, you should be able to stop in the distance lit by your headlights.
- Where street lighting is provided, you will be able to see further, and, if it is appropriate, drive faster.
- At night you are likely to be more tired and your responses slower – give yourself an extra safety margin by keeping your speed down.
- Use your lights to see and to make yourself seen. Avoid dazzling other road users.

Avoid dazzling other road users

- For the regulations governing the use of lights at night see **11 Rules and regulations**.

Overtaking at night

- When you overtake at night you need to be cautious. You may not have seen other road users and you may not have seen bends or obstructions in the road ahead.

- Only overtake if you are certain that the road ahead is clear. Follow the advice given in Overtaking earlier in this chapter (see pages 141–145), but take extra care because you can see less.

- Dip your headlights to avoid dazzling the driver of the vehicle in front while you are following and until you have overtaken it. Similarly, if you are being overtaken, dip your headlights as the other vehicle draws past you. If you are dazzled, slow down and be prepared to stop.

• If the vehicle in front is indicating right, do not overtake, even if you think the signal is on by error. Wait until it is cancelled before moving to overtake. The other driver may be intending to turn into a junction which you cannot see.

Motorways at night

• On motorways always use your headlights, even if the road is well lit.

• Dip your headlights if you are following other vehicles so that the light from your beam falls short of them.

Headlights and dazzle

• The lights of vehicles coming towards you may distract or dazzle you at night.

• If you are dazzled you should slow down or stop.

• Flashing your headlights risks dazzling the oncoming driver, making the situation doubly dangerous.

• The Highway Code says that flashing your headlights has only one purpose – to let the other driver know you are there.

• Make sure you dip your own headlights well before passing oncoming drivers to avoid dazzling them.

CORNERING

The way you approach and drive through a bend can
make an enormous difference to your safety. Managed
properly, bends should cause no problems. Managed
badly, you could end up in hospital or worse.

Tyre grip

When you corner you make great demands on tyre
grip.

• For anything more than the shallowest of bends you
  will have to lose speed, probably by braking, which
  requires tyre grip.

• Then you will need to steer round the bend, which
  puts a second set of demands on tyre grip.

• If you bring both sets of demands together – braking
  and steering at the same time – you may exceed the
  amount of grip available, and your car will skid.

Similarly, increasing your speed by accelerating puts
demands on tyre grip. Accelerating and steering at the
same time again puts two sets of demands on the tyre
grip, and a skid may result.

Minimise the risk of skidding by separating the
demands on tyre grip.

• Avoid accelerating or braking while you are steering.

• Avoid steering while accelerating or braking.

• The more slippery the road surface, the less it takes

to break the tyre grip. So, the more slippery the road, the gentler your actions must be and the more important it is to keep the different demands on tyre grip separate.

How to approach and go round a bend

When cornering:

- brake on the approach to the bend to get the right speed for the bend
- steer round the bend
- avoid braking while you are steering and avoid steering while you are braking
- don't increase your speed on a bend until the bend straightens out.

Losing speed on the approach to a bend

- You may be able to lose sufficient speed on the approach to a bend by easing back on the accelerator.
- However you do it, the important thing is to have the right speed for the bend before you start to turn.
- Of course, if you miscalculate and enter a bend at too high a speed, you might have to brake as well as steer. You then run the risk of skidding.

Wherever you are, on bends or on the straight, you must always be able to stop in the distance you can see to be clear.

How to position your car for going round a bend

As you approach and go round a bend, you can make a big difference to what you see by where you position your car on the road.

• For a right-hand bend, you will get the best view of the road ahead if you approach and go round the bend well to the left.

• For a left-hand bend, you should approach and go round the bend in the middle of your lane. The best view would be from a position close to the centre

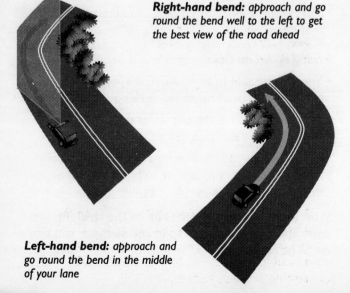

Right-hand bend: approach and go round the bend well to the left to get the best view of the road ahead

Left-hand bend: approach and go round the bend in the middle of your lane

line, but this would put you in danger of coming into
conflict with oncoming vehicles. So keep to the
middle of your lane.

Safety

Whatever position you are in, always be ready to
abandon it in the interests of safety.

• On a right-hand bend, pedestrians near the edge of
the pavement should make you cautious about
moving over to the left to get a better view.

• On a left-hand bend, oncoming traffic near to the
central line should make you select a course more to
the left.

COMMUNICATING WITH OTHER DRIVERS

Communicating clearly and correctly to other road
users is essential for safe use of the roads. The main
method of communicating is obviously signals, but
you should be aware that your position and speed are
also means of communicating your intentions to other
road users.

Only use signals in accordance with the Highway
Code. You should know thoroughly the Highway
Code sections dealing with driver's signals. The main
sections are rules 133–136, 150 and 153, **Signals to
other road users** and **The theory of safe and
responsible driving**, paragraphs 47–49.

Signals checklist

• Signal to help and warn other road users including
  pedestrians.

• Signal clearly and in plenty of time.

• Take care not to mislead other road users with your
  signals.

• Use the horn only to alert others to your presence,
  never to rebuke.

• Only use a headlight flash to warn other road users
  of your presence; do not use it for any other
  meaning.

• Never wave to pedestrians or any other road users to
  give way to them.

• Do not use informal signals.

• See **11 Signs and signals** for more on signals.

Warning signals: the horn and hazard warning lights

The horn

• The horn should be used to inform other road users
  of your presence.

• Do not use it when you are stationary unless a
  moving vehicle poses a danger.

• It should not be used to rebuke other drivers and it
  does not give you the right of way.

- At night, in built-up areas you must not use the horn between 11.30 pm and 7.00 am. Consider using a headlight flash instead.

How to use the horn

- Give a horn warning in plenty of time to allow the other road user to react.

- Don't use it as a substitute for steering, braking or accelerating your way out of danger.

- Last-minute use of the horn would suggest that you were not observing carefully enough.

Hazard warning lights

- Hazard warning lights (hazard flashers) enable you to warn other road users that you are stopped and causing a blockage or that there is a blockage ahead (on dual carriageways and motorways).

- When you switch on your hazard warning lights all your indicators flash at the same time.

- It is important to know where the hazard warning light switch is on your dashboard and what it looks like.

- While your hazard warning light is flashing, its symbol will flash on your dashboard. The hazard warning light symbol is a white triangle on a red background.

10 Other vehicles

This chapter covers the hazards associated with other vehicles that you are likely to meet on the road:
• long vehicles turning
• overtaking long vehicles
• service vehicles
• buses (and pedestrians using buses)
• vehicles with flashing lights
• markings on large goods vehicles
• spray from lorries
• motorcyclists
• the effects of crosswinds on other vehicles.

LONG VEHICLES TURNING

When a long vehicle is manoeuvring to turn, its initial move will often be to the opposite side of the available roadspace from the turn. This gives it more room for the turn. The driver behind the lorry can find this confusing. The lorry indicates one way and then moves the opposite way, leaving empty roadspace to the side.

• What the following driver must realise is that the lorry will pull back across this empty roadspace when it starts to make the turn.

• This can be very dangerous if the driver behind

moves up into the empty roadspace alongside the lorry. When the lorry turns it will collide with the vehicle on its inside and crush it.

• Lorries manoeuvring to make a tightish left turn will first move out to the right; those intending to make a right turn will move over to the left.

When you see a long lorry indicating to make a turn, or even slowing down so it looks like it might be making a turn:

• stay well back and give it plenty of room
• be prepared to stop
• do not move up into roadspace alongside the lorry, into which it might turn
• accept that the lorry's indicators are indicating the direction in which the lorry will turn
• be patient.

The manoeuvre the lorry makes in order to turn is sometimes called swan-necking, because the lorry first sweeps out and then pulls back sharply – like the shape of a swan's neck.

Expect lorries to move in the opposite direction to their eventual turn at:

• left or right junctions
• goods entrances and turnings into delivery yards
• crossroads
• roundabouts, especially mini-roundabouts.

OVERTAKING LONG VEHICLES

You need to take care when you are overtaking long
vehicles because it is difficult to see past them and
they take a long time to overtake because of their size.
When you are following a long vehicle that you wish
to overtake:

- stay well back from the long vehicle so that you can
  see clearly past it, and so that the driver can see you
  through the cab mirrors
- manoeuvre your car so that you can see past along
  both sides of the lorry, especially on bends
- when you can see clearly that there are no hazards
  ahead and there is an opportunity to overtake, make a
  final check behind, signal and then move out to
  overtake
- as you draw close to the rear of the lorry, assess
  whether it is safe to continue. If you have any doubt,
  pull back in behind the lorry
- if the lorry is travelling fast, expect wind turbulence
  as you draw past the cab.

Don'ts

- Don't get too close to the lorry before overtaking.
- Don't underestimate the time it will take you to get
  past a long lorry.
- Don't overtake unless you know the road ahead is
  clear

- Don't overtake in any of the places that the Highway Code says not to.

- Don't immediately move up into the space left by a vehicle in front of you that starts to overtake a long vehicle. It might need to abandon the attempt and drop back into its old place. Wait until it has overtaken before moving up.

SERVICE VEHICLES

Many service vehicles use the roads as their place of business, which makes their road behaviour different from the majority of other road users. For example:
- buses and coaches
- taxis
- trams
- road-sweepers
- gritters
- milk-floats
- ice-cream vans, hot-dog vans and other mobile shops.

Although their behaviour is different, it is usually predictable.

- When you see a bus you know it will be stopping to drop and pick up passengers, and if it has stopped you know that it will need to pull out after it has collected its passengers.

- Look for bus stops, pedestrians and the lengths of queues to anticipate what the bus is going to do.

- When you see a service vehicle, anticipate what it is going to do and alter your driving to accomodate it. Use the following checklist to help assess what it will do.

Service vehicle checklist

A service vehicle may:

- travel at a different speed from the rest of the traffic
- occupy different positions on the road
- pull up or pull out from the kerbside
- encourage pedestrians to cross the road
- conceal pedestrians stepping out into the road.

BUSES

Buses are big, long vehicles, so everything we have discussed about long vehicles also applies to buses. In addition, they pull in and pull out from the kerbside to pick up and drop off passengers. Help buses to move in and out of the traffic by remembering the importance of attitude – of courtesy, tolerance and helpfulness. Remember also the vulnerability of passengers.

Hazards to look for when you see a bus

Expect the bus to:
• travel at a different speed from the rest of the traffic
• pull over to the nearside as it approaches a stop, or to pull out to pass parked vehicles
• stop at bus stops and to pull out from them.

If you are following the bus:
• stay well back so that you can see what is happening ahead
• allow the bus to pull into and out of the traffic
• position yourself well away from the bus when you pass it at bus stops
• keep an eye out for pedestrians
• if the road is narrow, slow down.

If the bus is travelling in the opposite direction:
• anticipate its effect on the vehicles behind it
• watch for vehicles trying to overtake when it stops or pulls out
• consider whether it would be safer to position more to your nearside
• look out for pedestrians crossing to or from it
• if the road is narrow, slow down.

Expect pedestrians to:
• be in the road or about to cross near a bus or bus stop

- run across the road to catch the bus, or cross from the bus to the opposite pavement
- cross the road either in front of or behind the bus.

VEHICLES WITH FLASHING LIGHTS

You should know which vehicles have flashing lights, and the Highway Code advice on how to deal with them (rules 76, 77 and 152).

Blue flashing lights or sirens

Blue flashing lights are used on emergency vehicles such as ambulances, fire engines and police vehicles.

- Look and listen for emergency vehicles.
- Make room for them to pass.
- Pull over and stop if necessary but without endangering other road users.
- Slow-moving vehicles in the distance could mean an accident – drive slowly and be prepared to stop.
- Concentrate on the road. Don't let your attention be distracted by the accident.

Green flashing lights

Green flashing lights are used by doctors answering emergency calls.

- Give way as soon as you can but don't endanger other road users.

Amber flashing lights

Amber flashing lights are used by slow-moving vehicles (big loads, tractors, gritters, etc) or vehicles that have broken down.

• Drive carefully.

MARKINGS ON LARGE GOODS VEHICLES

You should know the meanings of markings on large goods vehicles. Look up and learn these in the Highway Code section on **Vehicle markings**.

School bus sign

• Follow the rules for buses and pedestrians, but be prepared for children to behave more unpredictably and erratically than adult pedestrians.

Long vehicles and trailers

• These must have 'Long vehicle' plates and red and yellow hazard stripes – allow plenty of time to overtake vehicles with these markings.

Vehicles carrying hazardous chemicals or dangerous goods

• These must have hazard warning plates – allow these vehicles plenty of room. (For more information about what to do if a lorry with hazard warning plates is involved in an accident, see Chapter 13.)

A load which overhangs the front or back of a vehicle

• A projection which overhangs by more than two metres (such as a jib or a crane) must be marked on the sides and end with triangular red and white striped projection markers.

• Keep well back from overhanging projections. Calculate your safe stopping distance from the end of the projection, not from the end of the vehicle.

MOTORCYCLISTS

Motorcyclists are more vulnerable than drivers of four-wheeled vehicles because they:

• are more affected by variations and irregularities of the road surface

• do not have a steel protective shell

• are easily blown off course by the wind or turbulence from large vehicles

In wet weather, the road surface becomes extremely hazardous for motorcyclists – metal covers and grills, road paint and the smooth tar around road repairs becomes very slippery.

• Always give motorcyclists room to manoeuvre to avoid these hazards.

• When you are following a rider, stay well back and give them plenty of space.

• Always allow a motorcyclist a full car width. Don't

muscle in on their space in slow-moving traffic.

- Look out for motorcyclists filtering past other vehicles in slow-moving traffic – give them enough space to manoeuvre round hazards in the road surface.

Look very carefully for motorcyclists before:

- pulling out at a junction
- turning into a left junction – check your nearside
- pulling across the other side of the road to turn into a right junction – check your offside, in front and behind
- pulling out to overtake.

The effect of wind on motorcycles

- Stay well back and give motorcyclists extra space when they are overtaking high-sided vehicles.
- Fast-moving, high-sided vehicles create a vacuum which pulls motorcycles towards them.
- As the motorcycle moves past the vehicle, it breaks free from the vacuum and may suddenly swerve outwards.
- Crosswinds buffet motorcyles more than cars, and can cause them to swerve in the same way.
- Crosswinds increase the vacuum effect alongside a high-sided vehicle, so that in windy conditions a motorcycle may swerve more sharply as it passes the front of the vehicle and breaks free of the vacuum.

THE EFFECTS OF CROSSWINDS ON OTHER VEHICLES

Although strong crosswinds will blow cars off course, other vehicles are even more likely to be buffeted. Those most likely to be blown about are:

• cyclists
• motorcyclists
• high-sided vehicles.

• In flat open country, keep a firm grip on the steering wheel to counteract the effect of crosswinds.
• Where vehicles move out from shelter, or where the wind is very gusty you should anticipate vehicles suddenly swerving, especially those in the high-risk categories.
• In these conditions give other road users plenty of room.
• If you wish to overtake, choose your place very carefully, and make sure there is room for the other vehicle to move sideways.

In windy conditions, places where you should expect vehicles to be blown off course are:

• on exposed sections of road – viaducts, hillsides, when leaving cuttings
• when leaving shelter, at the end of or at gaps in buildings, walls, fences, hedges, copses and woods
• when overtaking high-sided vehicles.

11 Rules and regulations

Safe use of the road depends on everyone knowing
and observing the rules and regulations in the
Highway Code. Many of these rules and regulations
have been introduced as apropriate for the subject
under discussion throughout the book. In this chapter
we look at the rules and regulations governing the
following areas:

• lane use
• restricted lanes
• lights
• parking and stopping
• speed limits
• occasions when you must stop.

LANE USE

Lane discipline is essential for the safety of road users.
The rules enable other road users to anticipate your
future moves and plan their own accordingly. They
also enable you to anticipate what others will do.

To use lanes properly you need to understand the
meaning of the various lines painted along the road.

Lines along the road

For illustrations see the Highway Code, **Road markings**.

• The **centre line** marks the centre of a single carriageway. The line is a single broken white line, with the gaps longer than the white markings. Generally only cross the centre marking to pass or overtake another vehicle or obstacle. Before you cross the centre marking check in your mirror for oncoming traffic. The centre line may also be marked with white studs (Catseyes).

• **Lane markings**, which divide the road into lanes, are also broken white lines but the markings are shorter and the gaps are longer. In roads with lanes keep between the lane markings and avoid straddling them. The lanes may also be marked with studs:
  – white studs between the lanes
  – red studs on the left edge of the road
  – amber studs next to the central reservation of a dual carriageway
  – green studs across lay-bys and side roads.

• **Hazard warning lines** are broken white lines that have long markings and short gaps, with markings longer than the gaps. They are placed on the approach to and alongside hazards. When you see hazard warning lines on the road, look for the hazard and be cautious. The Highway Code says do not

cross hazard warning lines unless you can see that
the road is clear well ahead.

- **Double white lines** are painted down the centre of
the road. They are of two types – where both lines
are solid and where one of the lines is broken. Where
the line on your side of the road is solid you must
not cross it except in the circumstances given below.
Where the line on your side of the road is broken,
you may cross it to overtake, if it is safe, providing
you are able to return to your side of the road before
reaching an unbroken white line on your side of the
road.

- Circumstances where, providing it is safe, you may
cross a double white line with an unbroken line on
your side of the road:
  - to get into or out of a property or a side road
  - to pass a stationery object blocking your lane
  - to pass a slow-moving vehicle travelling at less
    than 10 mph.

- **Edge markings** are solid white lines which mark the
edge of the road. They are broken at junctions, lay-
bys and driveways. On motorways edge markings
may have raised ribs to alert you to the fact that you
are moving off the carriageway.

- **Diagonal stripes (hatched markings)** mark out
areas that are used to separate traffic lanes or to
provide refuges for traffic turning right. Where the

line surrounding them is a solid white line, you must
not enter them except in an emergency. Where the
surrounding line is broken you may only enter them
if it is safe to do so. But remember the Highway
Code advice not to overtake at a road junction on
either side of the road.

Lane discipline

• Where there are lanes marked, keep within the
  markings. Avoid straddling central lines or lane
  markings unless you need to do so and it is safe.

• When you wish to overtake, use the **MSM PSL**
  procedure (See pages 57–58). Always check in your
  mirrors before you signal and always signal (if a
  signal is necessary) before you move.

• Do not change lane to overtake if it would cause
  another road user to change speed or direction.

• Where lanes go in different directions at junctions,
  try to get in the correct lane early on.

• See **9 Vehicle handling** for general advice on
  overtaking and **6 Different types of road** for lane
  use and overtaking on motorways.

RESTRICTED LANES

Parts of some roads are restricted for use by particular
road users. Car drivers either must not use these lanes
or must not use them at the stated times.

- These restricted lanes are cycle lanes, bus lanes and tram lanes.
- They are shown by road markings and signs.
- Bus and cycle lanes are marked by white lines along the road.
- Tramways may be marked by white lines or a different coloured or textured road surface.
- Signs show the hours of operation and any other conditions regarding the use of the lanes. If no hours of use are shown the restrictions apply all the time.

Tram lanes

Particular care needs to be taken with tram lanes.

- Trams are quiet and fast.
- Trams cannot be steered to avoid you.
- Trams overhang the tracks, so keep well away from tramways, especially on bends.

Restricted lane signs

Make sure you know the following signs dealing with restricted lanes in the **Traffic signs** section of the Highway Code:

- route to be used by pedal cycles only
- buses and cycles only
- trams only
- with-flow bus and cycle lane

- contra-flow bus lane
- with-flow pedal cycle lane
- cycle route ahead
- trams crossing ahead
- with-flow bus lane ahead
- bus lane on road at junction ahead.

LIGHTS

The Highway Code says that your lights must be clean and in working order, and your headlights must be properly adjusted so as not to dazzle other road users.

When to use your lights

Sidelights

- You must use sidelights from sunset to sunrise.

Headlights

You must use your headlights at night (defined as from 30 minutes after sunset to 30 minutes before sunrise):

- on roads without street lights
- on roads where the lights are more than 185 m (600 ft) apart
- on roads where the lights are out.

You must also use your headlights or front foglights in daylight if visibility is seriously reduced, which

generally means not being able to see for more than
100 m.

Dipped headlights

You should use dipped headlights:
- at night on lit motorways with a speed limit above
  50 mph
- at night in built-up areas unless the roads are well lit
- when you meet other road users to avoid dazzling
  them. Remember to dip your headlights before your
  lights could dazzle a driver you are following.

Dim-dip lights

If your car has dim-dip lights, use them instead of
dipped lights:
- in dull daylight
- at night in built-up areas with good street lighting.

Dazzle

If you are dazzled by oncoming headlights, slow down
or stop.

Use of lights on motorways

During the day

On motorways during the day:
- use your headlights if visibilty is reduced by fog,
  rain, snow or spray

- only use your foglights if visibility is less than 100 m
- you may use your hazard warning lights while moving to warn traffic behind of a hazard ahead. Switch them off when your warning has been observed
- use your hazard warning lights while stopped on the hard shoulder in an emergency. Also use your sidelights if visibility is poor.

At night

On motorways at night:
- use your headlights, even if the road is well lit
- dip your headlights if you are following other vehicles so that the light from your beam falls short of them
- only switch off your headlights on a motorway if you have had to stop on the hard shoulder because of an emergency. Leave your sidelights on, and switch on your hazard warning lights.

PARKING AND STOPPING

Parked vehicles are hazardous for other road users if they restrict their vision and space. They can be very hazardous for pedestrians, particularly children. Before you park, think how your vehicle will affect other road users. Make sure you are familiar with the

Highway Code rules 137–146 which cover waiting and parking.

The Highway Code advises drivers to park off the road or in a designated parking place. If you park on the road:

- park as close to the side of the road as possible
- leave plenty of space for other road users who have already parked to get out, especially vehicles displaying a disabled person's badge
- make sure before you open a door that you will not open it into the path of another road user – either on the kerb side or the road side
- where possible, and especially for children, leave the vehicle by the doors opening on the path side
- always lock your vehicle.

When you park you must

- switch off your headlights
- switch off your engine
- make sure your handbrake is on.

You must not

- stop on the carriageway of a motorway
- stop on a pedestrian crossing or within the zig-zag lines
- stop on or obstruct a cycle, bus or tram lane during the hours of operation

- stop on a clearway or urban clearway during its hours of operation

- stop on a road marked with double white lines, even if one line is broken.

- park on yellow lines or red routes during the specified restricted times

- park in parking spaces reserved for specific users, such as residents or disabled persons (orange badge holders).

You may stop to pick up or drop off passengers on an urban clearway or where there are double white lines, providing there are no other restrictions in force. You must not stop in a clearway. It is indicated by the 'No stopping' sign.

Obstructing other road users

The Highway Code says do not park where you would endanger or inconvenience other road users. In rule 140 it gives a list of places where you would obstruct other road users if you parked. You should know this list for the test.

Parking at night

- At night, you must park facing in the direction of the traffic so that your rear reflectors are lit by the headlights of vehicles driving on your side of the road.

• It is illegal to park facing the other way.

Cars may be parked without sidelights on the road at night providing the speed limit is 30 mph or less, and the car is parked in the direction of the traffic flow, close to the kerb and more than 10 metres (32 ft) from a junction or the car is parked in a recognised parking place.

Trailers must not be parked on the road at nights without lights.

Parking restrictions

Parking restrictions are imposed by road markings (usually yellow lines along the edge of the road or white broken lines round a bay) and parking restriction signs. These are covered in **12 Signs and signals**.

SPEED LIMITS

Every stretch of public highway is covered by a compulsory maximum speed limit.

• The limits are indicated by traffic signs, street lighting and the type of road.

• Speed limits vary according to the vehicle as well as the road.

The speed limits give the legal maximum speed, not

the safe speed. The safe speed for a stretch of road
depends on the conditions. It will often be below the
legal speed limit.

- Where there is a speed limit sign, the speed limit
  applies from the sign.

- You must not exceed the speed limit once you have
  passed the sign. This means you should slow down
  before you reach it.

The national speed limit

The national speed limit varies according to the type
of road and the type of vehicle. The national speed
limit applies, unless signs say otherwise.

The national speed limits for cars, car-derived vans and motorcycles

Areas where there is street lighting and no other speed signs	30 mph
Single carriageways	60 mph
Dual carriageways	70 mph
Motorways	70 mph

Note

- The presence of street lighting imposes a compulsory
  speed limit of 30 mph on its own, without the need
  for a 30 mph sign.

- The 30 mph limit in areas with street lighting does not apply if there are signs showing other speed limits. The speed limit given on the signs is the one that applies.
- The maximum speed on single carriageways is 60 mph, not 70 mph.

The national speed limits for cars towing caravans and or trailers

Areas where there is street lighting and no other speed signs	30 mph
Single carriageways	50 mph
Dual carriageways	60 mph
Motorways	60 mph

Speed limit signs

You must not exceed the speed limit given on a sign. A 20 mph sign may mean that, in addition to the speed limit, traffic calming measures are in operation, so expect speed humps and chicanes (see pages 103–104). See the Highway Code, **Traffic signs**.

Note that a blue circular sign imposes a minimum speed requirement. You must not go slower than this speed unless it is unsafe or impractical. The end of a minimum speed requirement is shown by the same sign with a red diagonal bar across it.

Road work signs

In addition to permanent signs, temporary speed limit signs at road works must also be complied with. An illustration of one is shown here.

OCCASIONS WHEN YOU MUST STOP

You must stop in the following circumstances:
• after an accident in which you are involved
• at a red traffic light
• when instructed to do so by a police officer or traffic warden
• when instructed to by a school patrol
• when a road works stop/go board shows stop.

12 Signs and signals

Signs and signals is an important topic, so make sure you allow yourself enough time to study and memorise the relevant sections in the Highway Code.

Learn the Highway Code sections on **Light signals controlling traffic**, **Signals by authorised persons**, **Signals to other road users**, **Traffic signs** and **Road markings**. You must be able to explain:

- different types of road signs – ie signs giving orders, warnings, information, etc
- what individual road signs tell you about the road ahead
- different types of signs showing speed limits
- motorway signs
- light signals and signals used by people authorised to control traffic
- road works signs
- how to use signals correctly to give information to other road users
- road markings
- rules and regulations shown by road and traffic signs.

Remember that other topics in the theory test also require a knowledge of traffic signals, road signs or markings.

TYPES OF ROAD SIGN

There are three main types of road sign. Each has a
different shape. Learn these shapes and what they
mean. Colour adds further meaning to signs giving
orders and giving information.

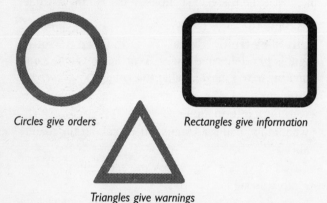

Circles give orders   Rectangles give information

Triangles give warnings

Signs giving orders and warnings also use symbols to
convey meaning. Symbols are a quick way to convey
information, as long as you understand what they
mean. Some signs also have plates which add
information about meaning. Look up these signs with
plates in the Highway Code:

• no vehicles
• pedestrians in road ahead
• school crossing patrol
• danger: hidden dip.

Signs that give orders

There are two types of signs
giving orders.

*Red circle – what
you **must not** do*

- **A white circle with a red
  border** tells you what you
  MUST NOT do. (The
  exceptions are 'Stop' and 'Give
  way' signs, which are a
  different shape for emphasis.)

- **A blue circle** tells you what
  you MUST do.

Look up and learn the
following signs:

*Blue background –
what you **must** do*

Prohibitive
- No right turn
- No overtaking
- No motor vehicles except for access
- Stop
- Give way

Positive
- Ahead only
- Pass either side
- Turn left ahead
- Keep right
- Mini-roundabout – give way to traffic from the right.

Memorise signs by learning a few at a time. You may find it easier to learn a group at a time, such as:

• all signs which **restrict access** for motor vehicles
• all **stop signs**
• all signs that **restrict stopping and parking**
• all signs that deal with **direction of travel** and turning.

Signs that give warnings

Most warning signs have a white triangle with a red border. As with signs giving orders, you will find it easier to memorise them if you arrange them in groups and learn them a few at a time, for example:

• all warning signs **for pedestrians**
• all signs that give **warnings about the road surface**
• signs for different **types of level crossing**.

Look up and learn these signs that warn about the road surface:

• uneven road
• slippery road
• ford
• ice
• risk of grounding
• humps for $1/2$ mile
• soft verges.

Signs that give information

Signs that give information are generally rectangular. There are three main groups:

- **direction signs** – mostly blue, green or white with a black border
- **general information sign**s – mostly blue (but remember motorway information and direction signs are also blue)
- **road work signs** – mostly yellow or red.

Direction signs

The colour of direction signs gives important information about the route:

- signs on motorways – blue background
- signs on primary routes (ie main roads to principal towns) – green background
- signs on smaller roads to local places – white background and black border
- signs giving tourist directions – brown background
- signs giving temporary directions about diversions – yellow background.

Signs that are confusing

Some signs look similar but have very different meanings. Certain signs are commonly misunderstood or confused with others. The theory test is designed to check these common confusions and mistakes, so take care not to mix them up.

Look up and learn:

- 'Stop' and 'Give way' signs and the rules that apply to them

- signs giving orders about turning or direction – all the circular signs with red borders which prohibit turning, and all the blue circular signs with arrows which give instructions about which way to go

- 'One way' and 'Ahead only' – you may go in only one direction in a one-way street, but you can turn off to left or right. You MUST go straight on at a junction or traffic lane marked 'Ahead only' – you cannot turn left or right.

- signs showing pedestrians: the different triangular warning signs, and the circular 'No pedestrians' order sign

- 'Give way to oncoming vehicles' and 'Priority over oncoming vehicles' – traffic travelling in the direction of the small red arrow must give way

Restricted access signs

- 'Two way traffic straight ahead' and 'Two way traffic crosses one way road'.

Do not confuse the Ring Road and Holiday Route signs which are used as route markers. These are not all shown in the Highway Code:

- ring road on primary route – white R on green square background, yellow border

- ring road on non-primary route – black R on white square background, black border

- holiday route – black HR on yellow rectangular background, black border.

Speed limit signs

You must be clear about the exact meaning of all speed limit signs. Look up and learn all the maximum and minimum speed limit signs, including the 'National speed limit applies' sign. The national limit varies with the type of road and the vehicle. Look up and learn the speed limits table in the Highway Code. If you are asked a question about a speed limit sign, you must choose the answer which is most accurate.

SIGNALS TO CONTROL TRAFFIC

You must understand the signals that are used to control traffic. These fall into two broad groups: light signals, and signals used by people authorised to control traffic.

Light signals

You must understand and comply with:
• traffic lights
• pedestrian crossing lights
• motorway light signals
• warning lights at level crossings, airfields, fire stations and lifting bridges.

Where there is a sequence of light signals, as at traffic lights, you must know exactly what each phase in the sequence means, and what phase will follow it.

Traffic lights

These are red, amber and green. Look up and learn the sequence of traffic lights in the Highway Code section on **Light signals controlling traffic**.

A RED light means:
• stop at the stop line.

An AMBER light means:
• the lights are about to turn RED
• stop at the stop line
• you may continue only if you have already crossed

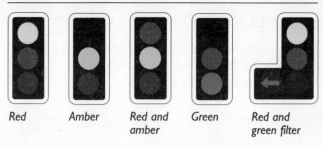

Red   Amber   Red and   Green   Red and
                    amber   green filter

the stop line, and to pull up sharply might be dangerous.

RED and AMBER lights mean:
• stop
• do not pass through or start
• wait until the lights turn GREEN.

Remember that a GREEN light does not necessarily mean you can go. You should wait or give way:
• if your way ahead is blocked by other traffic (otherwise you may find yourself stuck right in the middle of the junction when the lights change again)
• if pedestrians are crossing.

Filter signals

Many people get confused by the green arrow filter signals for left-hand or right-hand lanes.
• If the green filter arrow is showing and the way is clear, you can go in that direction, whatever the other lights are doing.

• If the filter is NOT showing, follow the other lights.

In the right-hand lane at traffic lights with a right-hand filter light, you can go when you see:
• red and green filter
• amber and green filter
• red and amber, and green filter
• green and green filter
• green alone, no filter.

You must not go when you see:
• red alone, no filter
• red and amber alone, no filter.

Look up and learn the difference between the road signs used on the approach to traffic lights:
• the warning sign for traffic lights ahead
• the sign meaning traffic lights out of order.

Light signals at pedestrian crossings

Traffic lights for vehicles at pedestrian crossings follows the same sequence, except that at pelican crossings:
• The red light is followed by a flashing amber light, not by red and amber lights together.
• At this point, pedestrians see a flashing green man to warn them the lights are about to change.
• You MUST give way on a flashing amber light to pedestrians crossing or about to cross.

Flashing red lights

Warning lights may mark level crossings, fire stations, lifting bridges and airports. The sequence and meaning of the amber and flashing red lights is always the same.

The amber light warns that the flashing red lights are about to come on. You MUST stop at flashing red lights, whether or not you can see or hear any danger.

PEOPLE AUTHORISED TO CONTROL TRAFFIC

Four groups of people are legally authorised to control traffic. You MUST comply with their signals. They are:

Police officers and traffic wardens using arm signals

- Learn the arm signals illustrated in the Highway Code.
- A police officer or traffic warden may signal a line of traffic to stop with one hand, and beckon another line of traffic to move forward with the other.
- If a police officer or traffic warden is directing traffic at a junction with traffic lights, you must stop at the stop line, as you would normally. If you creep forward you may block the junction and make the person controlling traffic less visible to others.

Road workers using stop/go boards

• Over short lengths on single carriageway roads, road workers may use stop/go boards instead of temporary traffic lights.

• A manually operated temporary stop sign has the same red hexagonal shape as a permanent stop sign, but the border is grey and circular.

School crossing patrol using a crossing patrol sign

• Learn the crossing patrol sign.

• Watch out for school crossing patrols near schools at times when children are arriving or going home.

• Be prepared for the patroller to signal you to stop.

Police officer in a patrol car

• If the patrol car is behind you, the police officer will flash the headlights, point to the left, and indicate to the left.

• You must pull over and stop if signalled to do so by a uniformed police officer in a marked police car.

GIVING SIGNALS TO OTHER MOTORISTS

You should know how to signal information to other motorists accurately using:

• indicators

• arm signals

• flashing lights

• horn.

Indicators and arm signals

Indicators are to give other road users information
about a driver's intentions. Learn the arm signals in
the Highway Code. Arm signals are rarely needed by
car drivers, but can be very useful to clarify meaning.
Always assess the situation.

If an indicator signal could be misunderstood

Decide when to give the signal
• If you wish to pull up on the left just after a left
  junction, or to pull up on the right just after a right
  junction, wait until you have passed the junction and
  then signal. If you signal before the junction, other
  road users may think you intend to turn into the
  junction.

*Consider whether an arm signal as well will
help make your intentions clearer*
• You are in a narrow road and want to turn right into
  a driveway. You need to move to the left to start the
  tight right turn. Indicate right and give a turning right
  arm signal.

• You wish to pull in and park on the left, just before a
  left junction. Indicate left and give a slowing down
  arm signal.

• Never base decisions on other drivers' indicator
  signals alone. People forget to cancel indicators.

• Look for changes in the other vehicle's position and

speed to confirm the signal, before you act. For
example, if you are waiting to pull out on to a main
road and an approaching vehicle signals an intention
to turn left, wait until you can see the vehicle really
is turning before you start to pull out.

• If for any reason you cannot use your indicators, you
  must know and be able to use arm signals.

• You must also recognise and respond to arm signals
  given by motorcyclists, cyclists, and horse riders.

• AVOID informal signals, such as waving pedestrians
  across the road. Your signal may be taken to mean
  that the whole road is safe to cross, and you may
  unintentionally draw pedestrians into danger from
  other vehicles that you cannot see.

Horn and flashing headlights

• Only use your horn or flash your headlights as a
  warning to let other road users know you are there.

• Use the horn cautiously – children on cycles and
  animals may be easily startled.

• You must not use the horn between 11.30 pm and
  7 am in built-up areas.

• You must not use it when stationary, except if you
  are in danger from a moving vehicle.

There is no other officially recognised use of the horn
or headlights. Be very wary when another driver
flashes his or her headlights. Although this is often

used to mean 'come on', the signal may not be meant
for you, and the person signalling may mean
something completely different. Within the rules of the
Highway Code, the following uses of horn or
headlights are not correct:

• using the horn to rebuke another driver for cutting in

• flashing headlights to invite another vehicle to move
  forward

• flashing headlights to tell a vehicle in front to move
  over in the fast lane on the motorway

• using the horn to attract the attention of a friend on
  the pavement.

ROAD MARKINGS

You must understand and comply with markings
painted on the road. There are three main types of road
marking. Look up and learn the section on **Road
markings** in the Highway Code.

• Across the carriageway – a solid line means you
  MUST stop at the line, and a broken line means you
  MUST give way.

• Lines along the edge of the carriageway or on the
  kerb – yellow lines and marked out parking or
  loading bays tell you about parking and loading
  restrictions.

• Lines along the carriageway – white lines and
  hatched areas tell you where you can and cannot

overtake safely, and there may be lines and studs
which give you information about the edges of the
carriageway.

The Highway Code also shows other road markings.
Apart from the warning mark for 'Give way', you are
most likely to meet these markings in towns.

Remember that road markings tell you about hazards,
and a good guide is the more paint, the more
important the message. Ignoring important messages is
likely to increase the potential danger to yourself and
other road users.

Stop and give way lines

Look up and learn the difference between lines across
the carriageway:

Stop line at stop sign	Thick solid white line
Give way to traffic on major road	Double broken white line
Give way at mini-roundabout	Single thick broken white line
Give way at roundabout	Single thin broken white line
Stop line at traffic lights	Single thin solid white line

Waiting restrictions

Yellow lines along the edge of the road mean there are parking restrictions. Usually the more paint, the greater the restrictions. You cannot park during restricted times but you can stop to load or unload, or pick up or set down passengers, unless there are also loading restrictions.

- A double yellow line along the edge of the road means no parking at any time including Sundays and bank holidays.
- A single yellow line along the edge of the road means no parking during the times on the sign.
- A broken yellow line along the edge of the road and a parking bay marked out with a dotted white line also mean there are parking restrictions.

By January 1999 the system will be simplified and the broken yellow line phased out.

Learn the 'No waiting' symbol shown on the plates where parking is restricted. This symbol also appears on signs at the start of meter and parking voucher zones, and on temporary 'No waiting' signs.

Loading restrictions

Yellow lines painted on the kerb, or a bay marked out by a dotted white line with the words 'LOADING ONLY' mean there are loading restrictions.

- Where you find these markings, look for a nearby plate, or the sign at the entry to the restricted zone, which will tell you the exact waiting or loading times.

- An arrow on the sign shows in which direction the restriction applies.

- The restrictions apply EVERY DAY OF THE YEAR unless the signs say otherwise.

- If there are no restricted times or days shown on the loading bay sign, the bay may be used for loading at any time.

Markings along the carriageway

Lines painted along the carriageway mark the middle of the road or divide it into lanes. Learn these markings in the Highway Code and look up and learn the rules that apply to carriageway markings (rules 83–87). These are shown under the relevant illustrations. The rules are about when you may and may not overtake, or enter marked areas:

- You MUST NOT cross a double white line when the line nearest to you is unbroken, except to turn right, or to move out round a stationery obstacle, and only if it is safe to do so.

- If the single broken line in the middle of the road changes from short markings to long markings with short gaps, you are approaching a hazard (for example, a bend, junction or concealed dip). Do not cross the hazard warning line – slow down until you can see that the road ahead is clear.

- White diagonal stripes or chevrons on the road are there to increase safety. They either separate lanes of traffic or protect traffic turning right. If the marked area is bordered by a solid white line, you MUST NOT enter it except in an emergency. If the area is edged by a broken line, you may only enter if it is safe to do so.

- If you are travelling on a carriageway divided by road markings into two or more lanes, you MUST NOT overtake on the left unless you are turning left in a one-way street, or traffic is moving slowly in queues.

Markings along the edge of the carriageway

- The edge of the carriageway on larger roads may be marked by a solid white line.

- This changes to a broken line where there is a junction, driveway or traffic lane leaving the main carriageway.

- Colour-coded reflecting studs may also be used to mark the edge of the carriageway, to increase visibility at night or in bad weather.

The colour code is the same on all roads, including motorways. Learn what the colour code means.

- Red studs mark the edge of the carriageway.

- Green studs mark a sliproad entrance or exit, or layby.

- Amber studs mark the central reservation on a motorway or dual carriageway.

- White studs mark the middle of road, or lines between traffic lanes.

Other road markings

Learn the other road markings in the Highway Code, and look up and learn the rules that go with bus stops (rule 140), bus lanes (rule 97) and box junctions (rule 113). These rules indicate when you may and may not enter, stop in or park in areas restricted by markings.

Zig-zag lines

Zig zags are painted along a section of road that is used regularly for crossing. Both people on foot and vehicle drivers need a good clear view of the road at these points. If you park on the zig zags, you block drivers' view of pedestrians about to cross and pedestrians' view of approaching cars. You could cause an accident.

Two types of zig-zag markings are painted along the edge of the carriageway:

- yellow zig-zags mark school entrances (there may also be a school warning sign and flashing amber lights before the school)

- white zig-zags mark the approach to pedestrian crossings.

- You MUST NOT park anywhere on zig-zag lines, not even for a few moments to set down or pick up children at a school entrance.

- You may only park before or after the zig-zags.

SIGNS AND SIGNALS ON MOTORWAYS

Signs that appear on motorways are blue. Directions signs on boards and the overhead gantries are shown in the Highway Code, **Direction signs**. Other motorway signs shown in **Information signs** are:

- start of motorway – motorway regulations start from this point

- end of motorway – motorway regulations end at this point

- service area sign – shows name of services, operating company and services available

- countdown markers – these appear at 300, 200 and 100 yards from the motorway exits.

Although you may not drive on a motorway until you have passed your practical test, you must show in the theory test that you understand motorway signs and the rules that go with them, and can respond to them correctly. Look up and learn the motorway direction signs in the Highway Code.

Gantry signs

• Downward-pointing arrows on gantry signs mean
  'Get in lane'. They indicate that the lanes will divide
  ahead and lead to different destinations.

• On the approach to complicated junctions, each lane
  may be signposted to a different destination.

• React to 'Get in lane' signs in good time.

• Arrows pointing upwards on gantry signs give you
  information about destinations.

• A vertical arrow shows the destination if you
  continue straight ahead on the motorway.

• A sloping arrow pointing upwards shows the
  destination if you leave the motorway at the next
  sliproad or junction.

Direction panels

• The number of the junction appears in white on a
  black square on blue direction panels and on gantry
  signs. It also appears on maps, so you can identify
  the turn-off you need before you start on a motorway
  journey.

• Approaching a turn-off, there are blue panels
  showing the distance to the sliproad or junction. If
  you intend to leave the motorway, you should move
  into the left-hand lane in good time.

Motorway light signals

Learn the motorway light signals in the Highway Code section on **Signals controlling traffic**. Motorway light signals are lit up to warn drivers when there is a hazard ahead. They are on a black background with an amber light at each corner. Top and bottom amber lights flash alternately.

• Light signals appear on overhead gantries, or on boards on the central reservation or at the back of the hard shoulder.

• Signals on the central reservation or hard shoulder apply to all drivers.

• Signals on overhead gantries apply to vehicles in the lane beneath the signal.

Learn carefully the difference between the sign for 'Change lane now' (diagonal arrow) and the sign for 'Leave motorway at next exit' (right angled arrow).

You must understand and comply with signals that tell you to stop or change lanes. On busy motorways, overhead lane control signals can vary the number of lanes available to traffic travelling in each direction, so that, for example, there are three city-bound lanes open in the morning rush hour, but only two lanes at other times.

13 Accidents and breakdowns

You should know how to deal with accidents, breakdowns and other emergencies on different types of road. Because of the high speeds and greater danger, there are special safety rules for dealing with emergencies on motorways. You need to be clear about the differences between what you should do on the motorway and on ordinary roads. You need to know:

• what to do if you are first to arrive at an accident, and how to give basic first aid

• how to use hazard warning lights and a warning triangle to warn other drivers

• what must be reported, when, and to whom if you are involved in an accident

• how to deal safely with breakdowns, burst tyres, objects falling from vehicles, fire and other hazards.

WHAT TO DO IF YOU ARRIVE FIRST AT AN ACCIDENT

Look up and learn the Highway Code rules on breakdowns and accidents (rules 149–154) and the section in **Additional information** (paragraphs

87–92). If you arrive at the scene of an accident, follow these safety rules in order:

1 ASSESS the situation
- What are the immediate dangers?

2 Make the area SAFE
- Reduce the danger and warn others

3 Organise HELP
- Get someone to phone the emergency services if needed
- Give first aid if you can
- Get uninjured people clear of danger.

Assess the danger and try to make the accident area safe *before* you try to give help to people who are injured. If you don't, you are risking your own safety, and that of other drivers. If you follow the safety rules, your help may prevent further injuries or loss of life.

If anyone is seriously injured, you must make sure an ambulance is called as quickly as possible. Getting life-saving equipment on its way to a casualty is as important as giving emergency aid. Think of first aid as a bridge until trained help arrives.

1 Assess the situation
- The most immediate dangers are likely to be fire and collision.

- These could cause further injuries to casualties, helpers or other road users.
- If a lorry with a dangerous load is involved, there could be a danger of toxic liquid, dust or gas.

2 Make the area safe

- Remove fire hazards if possible.
- Ask people to put out cigarettes.
- Switch off engines.
- Warn other drivers.
- Use a warning triangle.
- Put on your hazard warning lights.
- Position someone to wave other drivers to slow down, if they can stand in a safe place to do so.

3 Organise help

- Make sure someone phones the emergency services, if they are needed, before you do anything else.
- Make sure you tell the services the exact location of the accident
- Tell them how many people are injured, and how seriously.
- Do not hang up until the operator tells you to do so – under stress, you may forget to give vital information.
- Get uninjured people clear of danger. The hard shoulder, carriageway and central reservation of

a motorway are not safe, so move people well on to the embankment if possible.

• Give first aid to casualties – see below.

HOW TO GIVE BASIC FIRST AID

Learn the information in the Highway Code section on **First aid on the road**. Assess the situation and make the area safe before you give first aid. If you don't have first aid training, there are still some basic things that you can do for people who are injured in an accident. It is vital to get an ambulance quickly to someone who appears to have stopped breathing or have no pulse. Before the ambulance arrives, breathing for the casualty can buy time and increase the chances of survival.

If someone is not breathing

• Remove any obstacles in the mouth (eg chewing gum).

• Tilt the head back and lift the chin. This makes sure the tongue is not blocking the airway.

• If breathing does not start, give artificial ventilation. Close the person's nose by pinching the nostrils together. Blow into the mouth until you see the chest rise.

• Stop and then repeat every four seconds until breathing starts.

If someone is breathing but unconscious

- Do not move the person unless they are in danger, as this could worsen a back injury.
- Keep a close eye on them until the ambulance arrives.
- If they stop breathing, give artificial ventilation.

If someone is bleeding

- Put firm pressure on the wound to stop the flow of blood. Make a pad using clean material if possible, and hold it in place with a length of cloth.
- Raise a bleeding limb to reduce the flow of blood.

Don'ts

- Don't move anyone who is injured, or trapped in a vehicle, unless they are in danger. You may cause further injury.
- Don't remove the helmet of an injured cyclist or motorbike rider – this might cause further injury. The exception is if the person is not breathing and you need to remove the helmet to resuscitate them.
- Don't give an injured person anything to drink, eat or smoke. This could make their condition worse. If a casualty is thirsty, moisten her/his lips with water.

Reassurance

- Give reassurance to casualties.
- Talk to them calmly.

- Keep them warm and comfortable with coats or blankets
- Don't leave them alone.

Know how to recognise signs of shock. Shock can develop after an injury because the body withdraws the blood supply from the surface to the core.

- The most visible signs of shock are a pale grey skin which feels cold and clammy, with sweating.
- If you think someone is in shock, lie them down, with their feet raised, if possible, to improve the supply of blood to the vital organs.
- Keep them warm, and do not let them move.
- Reassure them constantly and make sure someone stays with them to watch their condition.

LORRIES WITH DANGEROUS LOADS

A lorry or tanker involved in an accident is a potential danger that must be assessed immediately. It could be carrying dangerous goods. If so, it must have a hazard warning plate on the side and rear. There are two kinds of orange hazard plate:

- **an orange hazard information panel**

  This has:
  - a diamond symbol showing the type of hazardous substance
  - coded information for the emergency services
  - a telephone number for help and advice

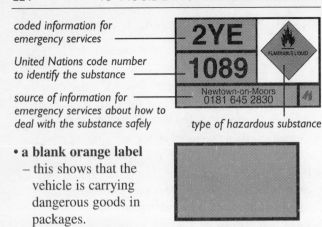

coded information for
emergency services

United Nations code number
to identify the substance

source of information for
emergency services about how to
deal with the substance safely

type of hazardous substance

- **a blank orange label**
  – this shows that the
  vehicle is carrying
  dangerous goods in
  packages.

If a lorry with dangerous goods is involved in an accident

- Note the information on the orange hazard warning plate *before* you phone the emergency services.
- Give the police or fire brigade as much information as possible from the orange plate, and information about the position and state of the lorry (eg if turned over, damaged or leaking).
- Warn people to keep well away from the lorry, especially if there is a letter 'E' or if there is a spillage.

WARNING OTHER DRIVERS

You must know how to warn other drivers correctly: switch on hazard warning lights and put up a warning triangle.

Hazard warning lights

Learn rule 134 about hazard warning lights. Even experienced drivers frequently use their hazard warning lights for the wrong purpose, such as parking on double yellow lines. There may be a test question to check that you understand the rules for using hazard warning lights correctly.

- Hazard warning lights may only be used if your vehicle is stopped and temporarily in the way of other traffic (ie in an emergency such as a breakdown).

- You may only use them while moving if you are on a motorway or unrestricted dual carriageway (ie where national speed limits apply), to warn vehicles behind that there is a hazard ahead.

- You must not use hazard warning lights for illegal parking.

These are examples of incorrect use of hazard warning lights:

- when parking for a few moments on the pavement to post a letter

- when driving slowly to look for a street in an area you don't know

- when parking on double yellow lines to call into a shop

- when towing another vehicle
- when driving slowly in very heavy rain that reduces visibility to a few yards.

Warning triangles

Carry a warning triangle in your car and know how to position it correctly at a breakdown or accident. Always use your hazard lights as well as a warning triangle, especially at night. You should position a warning triangle:

- **on an ordinary road**, 50 m (55 yards) before the hazard on the same side of the road
- **on a motorway**, at least 150 m (165 yards) before the hazard on the hard shoulder, NOT the carriageway
- **on a winding or hilly road**, before any bend or hill which is hiding the hazard on the same side of the road.

WHAT TO DO IF YOU HAVE AN ACCIDENT

If you are involved in an accident, you should:

- follow the safety rules to deal with immediate danger or injury (see above)
- collect information
- report the accident.

Collecting information

- Gather names and addresses of witnesses and car numbers of vehicles that were passing. Get details as soon as possible before people start to leave the scene.

- Exchange details (see below) with the other drivers involved. You must do this, but it is not necessary to enter into discussion about fault or blame.

- Record information – note down everything you can about what happened. Do this as soon as possible as important details are lost from memory even within a few hours.

- Draw a diagram showing how the accident happened.

- Take photographs if you have a camera.

Reporting accidents

Look up the Highway Code section on **The road user and the law**, and learn the rules that you must follow by law if you are involved in an accident in which a person or animal is injured, or property is damaged. You must:

- stop

- give your name and address, the vehicle owner's name and address and the registration number to anyone who has 'reasonable grounds' (ie, a good reason) for asking for them (such as other people involved in the accident, witnesses or the police).

If anyone is injured

• You must report the accident to the police in person as soon as possible, and in any case within 24 hours ('forthwith' in Northern Ireland) if the police did not take details at the time.

• You must produce your insurance certificate for the police within seven days if you did not produce it at the time.

When you must inform the police

You must call the police:

• if anyone is injured

• if you damage property but cannot find the owner to tell them.

You should also report the accident to your insurance company within 24 hours.

SAFETY RULES FOR DEALING WITH OTHER HAZARDS

Whatever the emergency, the same safety principles generally apply.

• ASSESS the situation.

• Decide what is needed to make it SAFE
  – reduce the danger if possible
  – get people clear of the danger
  – warn others.

• Get HELP.

If you have a breakdown

- Get your car off the road, or out of the way of other traffic as far as possible.

- If your car is in a dangerous place, get passengers out of the car and well away from the danger.

- Warn others – if your car is causing an obstruction use your hazard warning lights and warning triangle.

- Get assistance if necessary from the police or a breakdown service.

These general safety principles apply to all situations, but below you can see how the exact rules vary according to the type of road or circumstances.

On a motorway

- Get your car on to the hard shoulder if possible.

- Get passengers out of the car on to the embankment if you can do so without crossing the carriageway.

- Switch on your hazard warning lights.

- Put up a warning triangle on the hard shoulder at 150 m (165 yards) before the hazard.

- Go to the nearest emergency telephone and ask for help.

On a dual carriageway

- If the dual carriageway has a hard shoulder and emergency telephones, follow the rules for motorways.

- If not, get your car off the carriageway on to a verge or lay-by if possible.

- Switch on your hazard warning lights.

- Put up a warning triangle at 50 m (55 yards).

- Go to a phone and ask for help.

On a level crossing

- Get everyone out of the vehicle and well clear of the crossing.

- If there is a railway telephone, phone the signal operator.

- Do what the signal operator tells you. If no train is due, you may be told to get help and move the vehicle.

- If you cannot move your car and have to wait for help, warn other road users with hazard warning lights and a warning triangle.

If you have a puncture or burst tyre while moving

When a tyre is punctured or burst, it loses its grip on the road. This can cause your vehicle to swerve or skid. This will happen gradually if it is a puncture, or suddenly if the tyre bursts.

- Don't brake sharply. This reduces tyre grip further.

- Let the car roll to a stop, or brake as gently as possible.

- Keep a firm hold on the steering wheel and try to steer a straight course.

- Come to a stop gradually, at the side of the road and out of the way of other traffic if you can.

Driving a car with a flat tyre will damage the tyre and the wheel rim. Move your car only if you have to. Move it slowly and only the minimum distance necessary to put yourself out of danger.

- Move your car to a safe place before you attempt to change the wheel.

- Never try to change a wheel on the carriageway of a road.

- Get help if you are in any doubt about what to do.

- Only change a wheel yourself if you know exactly what to do and can follow the vehicle handbook instructions.

- On a motorway, walk to the nearest emergency telephone and ask for assistance.

- Never try to change a wheel on the hard shoulder, on the slip road, or anywhere else on a motorway. There is a risk that another vehicle may run into you at high speed.

If an object falls from your car

- On an ordinary road, stop in a safe place and pick it up as soon as possible.

• On a motorway, DON'T stop. Drive on to the next
  emergency telephone and tell the police.

If you see a large object fall from another car or from
the load of a lorry, and the driver doesn't stop, tell the
police. Don't try to pursue or attract the attention of
the other driver. Doing this may unintentionally create
another hazard.

If you think your vehicle is on fire

• Stop as quickly and safely as you can.

• Get everyone out of the vehicle.

• Get someone to phone the emergency services

• Do not open the bonnet. More air will fuel the fire.

• If you have a fire extinguisher, pull the bonnet
  release catch. Spray the foam into the space under
  the bonnet through the small gap made by releasing
  the catch.

• Never ignore a strong smell of petrol. Have it
  checked.

• Never ignore anything that looks like smoke. Stop
  and investigate immediately.

Index

Driving for Life

If you would like further preparation for the Driving
Theory Test, the National Extension College offers a
distance learning course, *Driving for Life,* which gives
you the best possible chance of passing the test.

The course is packed with information, questions,
activities and feedback. It also comes complete with
assessment tests and a study guide. Produced in
association with the Automobile Association and the
Associated Examining Board, the course includes two
computer-marked tests with individual guidance
feedback and a full mock theory test from the official
Driving Standards Agency question bank. The feedback
from this confirms your readiness to pass the test or gives
you detailed, targeted advice on how to do better.

You can contact the National Extension College by any of
the following methods.

Telephone: NEC Customer Services on 01223 316644
Email: nec@dial.pipexcom
Fax: 01223 313586
URL: http://www.nec.ac.uk
Write to: National Extension College, 18 Brooklands
Avenue, Cambridge CB2 2HN